Digital Togetherness in the Middle East and North Africa

American Society of Missiology Monograph Series

Chair of Series Editorial Committee, James R. Krabill

The ASM Monograph Series provides a forum for publishing quality dissertations and studies in the field of missiology. Collaborating with Pickwick Publications—a division of Wipf and Stock Publishers of Eugene, Oregon—the American Society of Missiology selects high quality dissertations and other monographic studies that offer research materials in mission studies for scholars, mission and church leaders, and the academic community at large. The ASM seeks scholarly work for publication in the series that throws light on issues confronting Christian world mission in its cultural, social, historical, biblical, and theological dimensions.

Missiology is an academic field that brings together scholars whose professional training ranges from doctoral-level preparation in areas such as Scripture, history and sociology of religions, anthropology, theology, international relations, interreligious interchange, mission history, inculturation, and church law. The American Society of Missiology, which sponsors this series, is an ecumenical body drawing members from Independent and Ecumenical Protestant, Catholic, Orthodox, and other traditions. Members of the ASM are united by their commitment to reflect on and do scholarly work relating to both mission history and the present-day mission of the church. The ASM Monograph Series aims to publish works of exceptional merit on specialized topics, with particular attention given to work by younger scholars, the dissemination and publication of which is difficult under the economic pressures of standard publishing models.

Persons seeking information about the ASM or the guidelines for having their dissertations considered for publication in the ASM Monograph Series should consult the Society's website—www.asmweb.org.

Members of the ASM Monograph Committee who approved this book are:

Susan Maros, Affiliate Assistant Professor of Christian Leadership
Fuller Theological Seminary

Sue Russell, Professor of Mission and Contextual Studies
Asbury Theological Seminary

RECENTLY PUBLISHED IN THE ASM MONOGRAPH SERIES

George Shakwelele, *Explaining the Practice of Elevating an Ancestor for Veneration*

Peter T. Lee, *Hybridizing Mission: Intercultural Social Dynamics among Christian Workers on Multicultural Teams in North Africa*

Digital Togetherness in the Middle East and North Africa

Deepening Relationships with Young Adults for Adventist Mission

CHANMIN CHUNG

A Dissertation Presented to the
Faculty of the School of Mission and Theology
FULLER THEOLOGICAL SEMINARY
In Partial Fulfillment of the
Requirements for the Degree
Doctor of Global Leadership

American Society of Missiology Monograph Series 75

◆PICKWICK *Publications* · Eugene, Oregon

DIGITAL TOGETHERNESS IN THE MIDDLE EAST AND NORTH AFRICA
Deepening Relationships with Young Adults for Adventist Mission

American Society of Missiology Monograph Series 75

Copyright © 2025 ChanMin Chung. All rights reserved. Except for brief quotations in critical publications or reviews, no part of this book may be reproduced in any manner without prior written permission from the publisher. Write: Permissions, Wipf and Stock Publishers, 199 W. 8th Ave., Suite 3, Eugene, OR 97401.

Pickwick Publications
An Imprint of Wipf and Stock Publishers
199 W. 8th Ave., Suite 3
Eugene, OR 97401

www.wipfandstock.com

PAPERBACK ISBN: 979-8-3852-1963-6
HARDCOVER ISBN: 979-8-3852-1964-3
EBOOK ISBN: 979-8-3852-1965-0

Cataloguing-in-Publication data:

Names: Chung, ChanMin [author].

Title: Digital togetherness in the Middle East and North Africa : deepening relationships with young adults for Adventist mission / by ChanMin Chung.

Description: Eugene, OR: Pickwick Publications, 2025 | American Society of Missiology Monograph Series 75 | Includes bibliographical references.

Identifiers: ISBN 979-8-3852-1963-6 (paperback) | ISBN 979-8-3852-1964-3 (hardcover) | ISBN 979-8-3852-1965-0 (ebook)

Subjects: LCSH: Digital media. | Digital communications. | Social media—Middle East. | Social media—North Africa. | Seventh-Day Adventists—Missions. | Mission of the church.

Classification: BV601.8 C48 2025 (paperback) | BV601.8 (ebook)

VERSION NUMBER 04/25/25

Abstract

This dissertation seeks to identify best digital media practices involving social media, instant messenger applications, and video communication platforms to strengthen Adventist frontline workers' online and offline relationship building and spiritual interactions with non-Christian young adults in the Middle East and North Africa for sharing God's redemptive love, grace, and peace. Part I of this study demonstrates from the literature that the use of digital media, social dynamics that include the attitudes of young Middle Easterners, and general trust-building factors may impact deepening relationships of trust and dialogue between workers and their young adult friends in the region. Part II explains how the three phases of exploratory sequential mixed methods—semi-structured interviews, a focus group, and an anonymous survey—were suitable for this phenomenological study.

    The findings display how digital media impacts relationship building and spiritual interactions between Adventist workers and their non-Christian young adult friends in the field. Digital media first catalyzes the process of learning about others and then creates a sense of care and togetherness as individuals continue to check on each other regularly without barriers of time and space. It also allows Adventist workers and non-Christian young adults to engage in deep spiritual conversations without security concerns or the risk of ruining relationships. In this vein, digital and in-person communication supplement each other to deepen relationships through trust and dialogue.

    This dissertation also describes brainstorming group activities. These were conducted in order to empower frontline participants to advance the above key findings to the eleven best digital media practices. Based on these, proposals are made for ways to apply the research findings to a larger group of Adventist workers in the region. Suggestions include (1)

Abstract

implementing three-day training sessions to prepare facilitators to conduct local group brainstorming activities and (2) following up with the local participants to identify tailored digital media model practices that can impact each field's young adult ministries.

Mentor: Dr. Alan Weaver

To my fellow gospel workers from
everywhere to everywhere.

To my wife, SuKyoung, to my sons,
JunYong and JunSu,
and to my God.

Contents

Abstract | v
List of Tables | xi
List of Figures | xii
List of Abbreviations | xiii
Acknowledgments | xv
Introduction | xvii

Part One: Communication Patterns and Social Dynamics

1 Digital Communication Patterns and Relationships | 3
2 Social Dynamics and Relationships | 17

Part Two: Field Research

3 Field Research Methods | 35
4 Findings: Impact of Digital Media on Relationship Building | 56
5 Findings: Impact of Digital Media on Spiritual Interaction and Limitations | 75
6 Reflections on Theoretical Constructs and Applications | 92

Part Three: Application

7 Application Strategy | 109
8 Concluding Thoughts | 132

Appendix A: Guides for Interview, Focus Group, and Survey | 139
Appendix B: Semi-structured Interview and Focus Group Participants Reference Sheet | 149

Contents

Appendix C: Survey Result Report | 152
Appendix D: Lecture Notes on Findings for Brainstorming Group | 165
Appendix E: Best DCM Practices for Young Adults | 174
Vita | 177
Bibliography | 179

List of Tables

Table 4.1: Field Research Questions and Categories | 59
Table 4.2: Relationship-Building Process | 60
Table 4.3: Impact of DCM on Relationship Building | 67
Table 5.1: Spiritual-Interaction Process | 76
Table 5.2: Most Used Spiritual Topics Survey | 80
Table 5.3: Impact of DCM on Spiritual Interaction | 82
Table 5.4: Limitations of DCM | 86

List of Figures

Figure 3.1: Conceptual Frame Flow Chart | 41
Figure 4.1: Creswell's Data Analysis Spiral | 58
Figure 4.2: Impact of DCM on the Relationship-Building Process | 73
Figure 5.1: Key Factors for Initiating Spiritual Interaction | 78

List of Abbreviations

AW	Adventist frontline worker
DCM	Digital communication media
IPC	In-person communication
MBB	Muslim-background believers
MENA	Middle East and North Africa
MENAUM	Middle East and North Africa Union Mission of Seventh-day Adventists
RQ	Research question
UNDP	United Nations Development Programme

Acknowledgments

I AM GRATEFUL FOR the many people who have supported this meaningful project and my growth as a leader through it. I express my earnest appreciation to the following people:

My wife, SuKyoung—your love, care, and encouragement made this project possible. You have been my faithful companion for this journey. Thank you for your sacrificial contribution to this work. I am here because of you.

My children, JunYong and JunSu, who have allowed me to focus on this project—I remember your prayers and sacrifices. You endured the absence of your dad at the beaches, camping, and board games. I love you both.

My mission colleagues in the Middle East and North Africa Union Mission of Seventh-day Adventists, especially Dr. Rick McEdward—you convinced me and others that this project was critical to nurture me as a leader and to advance the church's mission.

My ministry colleagues in the General Conference of Seventh-day Adventists—Dr. Oscar Osindo, Dr. Cheryl Doss, Enid Harris, and Laurie Wilson. You gave me full material, administrative, and emotional support.

My mentor, Dr. Alan Weaver—you have nurtured, refined, and stretched my ability as a researcher toward something I never could have imagined. You have spent considerable time polishing my potential until it shines.

My Fuller Theological Seminary professors: Dr. Susan Maros, Dr. Rob Dixon, Dr. Mark Hopkins, Dr. Andy Myers, Dr. Charles Fleming, and Dr. Ryan Bolger—I am grateful for your guidance, enthusiasm, and care. I am also grateful for my editor, Heather Campbell, who has sincerely walked with me to advance my dissertation to a higher level.

Acknowledgments

My cohort, Ekballo: Kirk Anderson, David Ingerson, Zewdie Jikamo, John Nicosia, and Mark Stevenson—you were not just cohort members, but also friends and prayer warriors who empowered me tremendously.

Introduction

"Can I have your Facebook name?" When the Egyptian man in his mid-twenties asked me this question, it made me nervous—I did not typically share my social media information with someone I had just met an hour ago. This was not a cultural or social norm with which I was familiar.

I had encountered this young man while I was walking on the riverside along the Nile in Cairo, Egypt, in 2011, after the Arab Spring. As we chatted, he and his friends explained their frustrations and concerns for the future. I was hoping to introduce them to our Seventh-day Adventist members in the city, so at the end of the conversation, I suggested that we exchange mobile numbers. However, instead of my phone number, they wanted my social media information. This request made me uncomfortable, but something about it stuck with me. Later, the stories I learned about the Arab Spring helped me to better understand the importance of social media in the lives of these young people.

Since that encounter with the young Egyptians on the riverside of the Nile, I have had many experiences in different Middle Eastern and North African (MENA) countries, such as Turkey, Tunisia, Morocco, Jordan, and United Arab Emirates. In all of these locations, I observed the role that digital media plays in relationship building for the younger generation. As I met more non-Christian young adults in such places as the buzzing cafés on Istiklal Street in Istanbul or Habib Bourguiba Avenue in Tunis, these individuals often expressed a desire to continue our interactions on digital media. These encounters happened over and over again; only the names of the preferred digital platform varied—from Facebook and Instagram to TikTok.

In 2018, I began my role as the media ministries director for the Middle East and North Africa Union Mission of Seventh-day Adventists (MENAUM). Initially, the team and I endeavored to define our primary

Introduction

audience and the appropriate mediums for reaching out to the audience. Throughout the discussion process, the mission leaders agreed that the church needed to prioritize inviting the younger generation. I then remembered the way that the young people I encountered in MENA engaged with one another—and with me—through digital media.

The media ministries team is a department of the mission office, and we had been able to employ digital technology to invite young people to Jesus Christ. But I was perplexed when I saw how many of our frontline workers and mission leaders considered the primary function of digital media to be that of a type of bulletin board or megaphone for information distribution. They did not consider the impact of digital media on their relationship building and interactions with non-Christian young adults in the field. Meanwhile, I observed some frontline workers who utilized digital media to build deeper relationships with their young adult friends. This left me with a puzzle: Is digital media a mere tool for content distribution and evangelism? Or can it be used for more?

The Seventh-day Adventist Church recognizes that digital technology is a useful tool for evangelism. Despite this, there is little that addresses how digital media is connected to the mission ecology that affects the transformation of the whole person in relationship. In this study, I sought to address that gap.

BACKGROUND

Over the past two decades, I have served as a television producer, creative director, television production manager, writer, social media outreach coordinator, leader of media ministries teams, and ordained minister. I have also served as an intercultural worker in the Middle East for more than twelve years. I now serve as the managing director of the Trans Media Group for MENA, which includes communication, television and radio, digital evangelism, publishing, and translation under MENAUM.

The mission oversees twenty countries in the region: Algeria, Bahrain, Egypt, Iran, Iraq, Jordan, Kuwait, Lebanon, Libya, Morocco, Oman, Qatar, Saudi Arabia, Sudan, Syria, Tunisia, Turkey, United Arab Emirates, Yemen, and North Cyprus. Although my study excluded high-risk countries such as Yemen, Iran, Libya, Syria, and the Kingdom of Saudi Arabia, the workers and young adults within the MENAUM territory served as the context of my research.

Introduction

Through this study, I desired to enhance Adventist workers' ability to cultivate deeper relationships of trust and dialogue with their young adult friends. In consideration of this purpose, it is critical to understand the impact of digital media on human life.

Manuel Castells, a leading sociology scholar on internet studies and network society, suggests that information technology in conjunction with social and economic turmoil creates a new world, including new social structure and culture.[1] In line with this, renowned missiologist Paul Hiebert explains that new technologies reshape fundamental worldviews.[2] Thus, it is vital to investigate the impact of digital media on the relationship-building processes and spiritual interactions among Adventist frontline workers and young adults in the post-Arab Spring era. It can help the church to better understand the attitudes and practices of the non-Christian young adults of MENA who are influenced by social upheavals and new digital media. A better understanding of this demographic may help Christian workers find more effective ways of building relationships and engaging in spiritual interaction with young adults in the region.

Missiologist for communication Viggo Søgaard proposes that in order to deliver the gospel effectively, Christian communicators and media professionals need to study changing contexts.[3] As a Christian media professional, I resonate with Søggard's statement. I argue that missiologists need to study the relationship between new media, changing views, and social relations within their mission ecology so as to minister to people under the influence of technology and its culture. Although the role of digital media in mission work in MENA is significant, and despite the fact that this technology has impacted the sociality of the younger generation in the region, Adventist workers serving there tend to focus on its function of content distribution and evangelism. However, an understanding of the media's relational nature is necessary for creating appropriate digital media strategies for the church's gospel workers who interact with their young friends every day.

Another key factor to remember is that the majority of MENA young adults are born Muslim. However, the wider Adventist mission has not paid much attention to reaching out to non-Christians, because people with similar Christian worldviews have been more receptive to

1. Castells, *Rise of the Network Society*, 337.
2. Hiebert, *Transforming Worldviews*, loc. 634.
3. Søgaard, *Research in Church and Mission*, 34–35.

Introduction

the Seventh-day Adventist's missional efforts than have non-Christians.[4] Through this research, I want to provide the Adventist Church in MENA with digital media model practices that can enhance Adventist workers' ministry of sharing God's redemptive love, grace, and peace with non-Christian young adults through relationship.

RESEARCH DESIGN

In this section, I present my research design. This includes the purpose of my research, my research goal, the central research issue, variables, research questions, the application intent question, research significance, assumptions, pertinent definitions, delimitations, and a dissertation overview.

Purpose

The purpose of this study is to enhance Adventist workers' ministry of sharing God's redemptive love, grace, and peace with non-Christian young adults in the Middle East and North Africa through online and offline relationships.

Goal

The goal of this study is to discover how digital media affects Adventist frontline workers' relationship-building processes with non-Christian young adults.

Central Research Issue

The central research issue of this study is to explore how communication patterns and social dynamics among Adventist workers and MENA young adults impact deepening relationships of trust and dialogue.

Research Questions

1. What are communication patterns, involving digital media, among Adventist workers and non-Christian young adults?

2. What are social dynamics, focusing on relationship building, among Adventist workers and non-Christian young adults?

---

4. Doss, *Introduction to Adventist Mission*, 340.

Introduction

3. What are critical elements for deepening relationships among Adventist workers and non-Christian young adults?

Applicational Intent Question

What digital media practices can be identified to strengthen Adventist frontline workers' relationship building and spiritual interactions with non-Christian young adults?

Significance

This study is important for my leadership, organization, and the field of missiology. First, I expect this research will strengthen my leadership ability to serve the Adventist Church's media ministries in the Middle East by enhancing my understanding of digital media's impact on Adventist workers' ministries. Second, I anticipate that this study will equip MENAUM and its frontline workers with digital media model practices for reaching out to young adults. Finally, I expect that this research will contribute to missiological literature by developing missiological implications of digital media and a response to the needs of the mission field amid technological and social change.

Assumptions

1. The specific Christian milieu in which this study takes place is within the faith assumptions of the Seventh-day Adventist Church.
2. I assume the usefulness of digital media model practices for the Adventist Church's mission work in the Middle East and North Africa.
3. I assume the importance of relationship building and spiritual interaction for frontline workers' in-field ministries.

Definitions

1. *Digital media*: Digital technology-based information infrastructure and platform, including the internet, social media, mobile phones, and websites that can transmit digitized content over computer networks.[5]

---

5. Gorrell, *Always On*; Manovich, *Language of New Media*.

Introduction

2. *Communication patterns*: Ways in which Adventist workers and non-Christian young adults interact and exchange information with each other through digital media. Communication patterns can include frequency of digital media use, attitudes, type of platforms and media, content, and interrelation with in-person communication.

3. *Social dynamics*: The interactions, relationships, peer networks, interpersonal roles, cultures, attitudes, and values individuals co-construct to organize their ecological settings.[6]

4. *Digital media model practices*: A set of applicable digital media usages that guides Adventist workers' use of the media for relationship building and spiritual interaction with young adults in the Middle East and North Africa.

Delimitations

1. This study is delimited to the cultural context of the locations within the Middle East and North Africa where Adventist workers reside and work.

2. This study is delimited to the theological, ecclesiological, and missional context of the Seventh-day Adventist Church.

3. This study is delimited to Adventist workers who work or used to work in the Middle East and North Africa.

4. The category of *young adult* is delimited to people between the ages of twenty and thirty-nine.[7]

OVERVIEW OF DISSERTATION

In the remainder of this dissertation, I exhibit the process that I used to study communication patterns involving digital media and social dynamics, focusing on relationship building and spiritual interaction among Adventist workers and their non-Christian young adult friends. This dissertation is divided into three parts. In part I, comprised of two chapters, I outline two primary literature review areas to discover the gaps and rationales for the field research. In chapter 1, I engage with the literature regarding the impact of digital communication patterns on human relationships, focusing on the sociality-related traits of digital media. In chapter 2, I investigate how the

---

6. Farmer et al., "Social Dynamics Management," 3.
7. Erikson, *Childhood and Society*.

Introduction

social dynamics of the attitudes and values of the younger generation in the post-Arab Spring period affect social relationships. I also examine how the social dynamics of general trust-building factors can impact the depth of relationships, which allows for spiritual interactions.

In part II, I focus on the field research process, including rationales, gaps, samples, data collection and analysis methods, and findings. In chapter 3, I describe my three phases of exploratory sequential mixed methods of research: (1) semi-structured interviews for forty Adventist workers, (2) a focus group comprised of five Adventist Muslim-background believers (MBBs), and (3) an online survey of fifty-one Adventist workers. I also describe how I endeavored to secure the validity and reliability of this study. In chapters 4 and 5, I explore key themes identified during the analysis of the research data. Then, in chapter 6, I reflect on the key findings in light of the literature review and applications.

In part III, I outline the process of applying my research findings to frontline workers through developing digital media model practices. In chapter 7, based on my research and the pilot brainstorming group, I suggest three-day training sessions to develop facilitators to organize and conduct local group brainstorming activities. In chapter 8, I conclude this research with key conclusions of this dissertation, recommendations, implications, and closing remarks.

SUMMARY

In this introduction, I provided an overview of the entire dissertation, and I described a structure of the study I conducted. This study was motivated by a desire to enhance Adventist workers' ministry of sharing God's love with non-Christian young adults in relationship via digital media.

This study was developed from an observation of Adventist workers' use of digital media for ministering to their non-Christian young adult friends in the Middle East and North Africa. Therefore, the central research issue of this study is to explore how communication patterns and social dynamics among Adventist workers and MENA young adults impact deepening relationships of trust and dialogue. This will allow me to understand Adventist frontline workers' usages of digital media and their experiences of relationship building and spiritual interaction with young adults in a post-Arab Spring context. Through this understanding, I intend to provide Adventist workers with concrete digital media model practices to minister in their contexts to the younger generation.

Part One

Communication Patterns and Social Dynamics

In their book, Networked *Theology: Negotiating Faith in Digital Culture*, Heidi Campbell and Stephen Garner state that digital media has altered social ecology through the ways in which it interrelates with values and relationships of humans.[1] This means that the ways in which humans communicate, think, behave, and build relationships interact with one another. Based on this point, in my research, I examined communication patterns and social dynamics as two critical factors that may impact deepening relationships of trust and dialogue among Adventist workers and non-Christian young adults. In part I of this dissertation, I describe the impact of communication patterns and social dynamics on relationships. This examination provides foundational knowledge for the field research.

In this research, digital media lies at the center of communication patterns that impact relationships among people in the Middle East and North Africa. In chapter 1, I thus examine the sociality-related traits of digital media and the effects of digital communication patterns on relationships. In chapter 2, I scrutinize Arab youth's attitudes, values, and culture as part of social dynamics that likely impact their relationship development. I also examine the factors of social dynamics that catalyze building trust in relationships, since a partial issue of this study is to explore how social dynamics impact deepening relationships of trust and dialogue among Christian workers and non-Christian young adults. Through this review, I surface gaps in the literature that I addressed through field research, which I discuss in part II.

1. Campbell and Garner, *Networked Theology*, 35–36.

1

Digital Communication Patterns and Relationships

SCHOLARS DEFINE DIGITAL MEDIA as a communication medium because it allows people to converse and maintain communities.[1] However, the media not only allows users to interact with others and sustain communities, but it also impacts relationship dynamics by changing the ways in which individuals communicate. Through digital media, the communication dance alters its rhythm so that people communicate more openly and transparently in a shorter time frame, which can affect relationship dynamics. One prominent example of this phenomenon occurred during the Arab Spring.

On December 17, 2010, the Arab Spring began when twenty-six-year-old Mohamed Bouazizi, a poor vegetable seller in Tunisia, set himself on fire in front of the governor's office to protest the political and police corruption that had led to the seizure of his vegetable cart.[2] Bouazizi's actions resonated with many who felt disenfranchised or victimized by a corrupt system, and shortly after Bouazizi's self-immolation, people in Egypt, Bahrain, Saudi Arabia, Libya, Yemen, and Jordan began to mobilize and take action.[3] Young people in the Middle East and North Africa (MENA), including Egyptians, actively utilized digital technologies such as social media and instant messengers to organize protests, and they also shared their ideas, thoughts, and feelings with others.

1. Castells, *Internet Galaxy*, 2–3; Dyer, *From the Garden*, 200; Kogut, *Global Internet Economy*, 3; Putnam, *Bowling Alone*, 184.
2. Ghanem, *Arab Spring Five Years Later*, 63.
3. Howard and Hussain, *Democracy's Fourth Wave?*, 22.

Part One: Communication Patterns and Social Dynamics

On January 18, 2011, in Cairo, Egypt, after the resignation of President Zine El Abidine Ben Ali in Tunisia, an urgent video was uploaded to YouTube and Facebook by twenty-six-year-old Asmaa Mahfouz. In it, she appealed to all Egyptians to participate in a grand protest at Tahrir Square.[4] She urged,

> If you think yourself a man, come with me on January 25th. Whoever says women shouldn't go to protests because they will get beaten, let him have some honor and manhood and come with me on January 25th. . . . Your presence with us will make a difference. . . . Talk to your neighbors, your colleagues, friends, and family, and tell them to come. . . . Go down to the street. Send SMSes. Post it on the net. Make people aware.[5]

On January 25, 2011, an enormous number of Egyptian demonstrators filled Tahrir Square in Cairo. Their mobilization against the government continued for eighteen days until the resignation of President Hosni Mubarak. In the past, Mahfouz's story—an ordinary young woman playing a critical role in a historic political event by using the power of digital technology to interact with others—would not have been imaginable culturally or technologically. This shows the potential for and influence of digital media on how people communicate with and relate to one other.

Decades earlier, when the *Voice of the Arabs* radio program encouraged Egyptians and Arab nations to fight against Western imperialism in order to regain the Suez Canal in 1956, Gamal Abdel Nasser, the second president of Egypt, was one of the main speakers.[6] He was a military general and the most powerful political leader at that time, and he was one of a few people who could access and control the radio broadcast. In comparison with Nasser's radio speech, Mahfouz's Facebook video was a departure from the patriarchal Arab tradition.

The contrast between these two events is striking, as it shows how digital media has changed communication patterns in MENA. For instance, consider the authoritarian male leader and traditional state-controlled media that existed in 1956. Now compare that to how in 2011, marginalized groups utilized social network sites and free-to-access digital media to express their disapproval of the established authorities and to network with people outside of their social boundaries.

4. Harlow, "It Was a 'Facebook Revolution,'" 61.
5. Mahfouz, "YouTube Video That Helped Spark."
6. Alahmed, "Voice of the Arabs Radio," 2–3, 12, 27.

Digital Communication Patterns and Relationships

Building on the above accounts, I argue that the shift from top-down to bottom-up communications shows something profound: digital media contributes to the change of communication patterns and relationships among people. Supporting my view, Egyptian communication scholar Rasha Abdulla argues that for a long period, digital media has equipped Arab youth, including Egyptian youth, to express their opinions freely.[7] Because of this, the media has increased a sense of connectedness among them, and their untraditional values were highlighted during the Arab Spring.[8] This means that even before the Arab Spring, digital media had already cultivated untraditional communication patterns in the region and enabled people in the region to speak out in challenge of their authoritarian leaders. For example, in Tunisia in 2007, a video uploaded by citizens showed the president's plane landing and taking off at shopping destinations in Europe for the benefit of his wife. The government then had to block and censor YouTube, Facebook, and other online platforms due to open disapproval of the president and his wife.[9]

Based on these examples in MENA, I now ask the following question: What was it that allowed digital media to have such influence on communication patterns and relationships among people? In order to answer the question, I examine the key sociality-related traits of digital media and how those traits impact relationships among individuals.

SOCIALITY-RELATED TRAITS OF DIGITAL MEDIA

A premise of this study is that communication patterns affect relationship development, since the ways in which individuals interact with others is a critical element of relationship building. In this sense, digital communication may also contribute to relationship development. This point necessitates an investigation into how communication patterns via digital media are connected to relationship development.

Moreover, in this research, digital media lies at the heart of communication patterns among individuals. Considering these points, digital media has three traits that facilitate closer social relationships: openness, connectivity, and real-life interplay.

---

7. Abdulla, "Egypt's Media," 9.
8. Abdulla, "Egypt's Media," 1, 9.
9. Howard and Hussain, *Democracy's Fourth Wave?*, 35–36.

Part One: Communication Patterns and Social Dynamics

First Trait: Open Communtication through the Internet

The first trait of digital media is open communication. Political scientist Robert D. Putnam proposes that a core characteristic of the internet is communication that enables individuals to be more candid and allows for more equality than do in-person meetings.[10] Manuel Castells argues that from the early stages of its development, the internet enabled people to practice freedom of expression, and this has become a predominant value of the media.[11] In the beginning of the internet era, users experienced unprecedented autonomy to express their thoughts and feelings online. If they had used another form of communication, they could have been censored by conventional media and governments. Although internet users experience more regulations and surveillance technologies today than they did when the media was first established, the culture of open communication has been solidified through long-time practice.

In a similar vein, Putnam attributes digital media's trait of open communication to anonymity. Because it does not always reveal information such as race, gender, and age about the users behind the screen, when people use digital media, they become more authentic, less partial, and less likely to be judged according to social status.[12] Putnam's claim indicates two important factors for open communication: First, when people use digital media for communication and they believe that no one knows their real identities—including social class, occupation, gender, education, religion, and location—such anonymity allows the users to share their honest feelings and opinions without social pressures or prejudices. Even if the opinions are against their social norms, they dare to share them because they are shielded by anonymity. Second, when digital media users do not know information about other users, communication becomes more respectful and egalitarian. For example, according to modern communication media expert Howard Rheingold, women experience less trouble in digital communications when their gender is not displayed than they do in offline interactions.[13] As a result, in patriarchal societies, female digital media users may feel less pressure and more respect when they anonymously express their opinions about gender equality.

10. Putnam, *Bowling Alone*, 186.
11. Castells, *Internet Galaxy*, 54.
12. Castells, *Internet Galaxy*, 186.
13. Rheingold, *Virtual Community*, 9–10.

Digital Communication Patterns and Relationships

Though I do acknowledge the importance of anonymity for authentic communication as a trait of digital media, placing anonymity at the center of open communication can be problematic. MIT technology and society professor Sherry Turkle explains the potential for cruelty as a result of anonymity in digital communications. Her argument is that anonymous open communication does not guarantee positive relationships among individuals in digital interactions.[14] If one shares his or her vulnerabilities transparently—albeit anonymously—with others, because of the facelessness of the person, strangers online can be unkind instead of offering respectful comfort, encouragement, or counsel.

While, according to Putnam, digital media's anonymity-based open communication trait enables humans to be more candid, respectful, and egalitarian, the same trait, according to Turkle, can be detrimental to people's emotional well-being. Based on this, I argue that the open communication trait of digital media can result in both positive and negative communication patterns and relationships. Moreover, although Turkle demonstrates valid points about the downsides of the anonymity of digital media, her critiques do not fully diminish the fact that this anonymity also encourages people to communicate authentically and vulnerably and that the act of venting can result in therapeutic relief.[15] This means that regardless of positive or negative reactions to open communication, the simple act of sharing one's secret burdens with others online can help alleviate stress. This demonstrates that people recognize digital media as a place to express themselves freely because it provides security as they share their thoughts about deep issues.

Though I value Turkle's points about the dangers of anonymity in internet communications, as a professional involved in digital media, I have observed numerous Middle Easterners and North Africans who hesitate to express their authentic selves if digital anonymity or confidentiality is not guaranteed. Research has shown that if a person's identity is obvious online, the authenticity of his or her opinion is questionable, because in those circumstances, many users tend to present the most desirable versions of themselves.[16] They may express only those thoughts and characteristics that can be harmonized with their cultural, social, and religious norms. For example, imagine that the late Steve Jobs, American

---

14. Turkle, *Alone Together*, 234–37.
15. Turkle, *Alone Together*, 232.
16. Mehdizadeh, "Self-Presentation 2.0."

Part One: Communication Patterns and Social Dynamics

entrepreneur and former CEO of Apple, is someone admired by the community. A person quite unlike Steve Jobs may endeavor to present himself or herself online in ways similar to Steve Jobs in order to gain the approval of others in the community.

This point reveals a significant impediment for spiritual interactions between Adventist workers and their non-Christian young adult friends. Sharing biblical messages with non-Christian young adults is a critical element of communication for Adventist workers. However, openly interacting with Christians about biblical subjects may not be desirable for non-Christians due to community expectations. In this case, anonymity or confidentiality of digital media can provide security for Christian workers as well as for non-Christians.

Luciano Floridi, an Oxford professor of philosophy and ethics of information, contends that displaying desirable social selves online does not mean forging inauthentic and ungenuine identities.[17] On the contrary, considering the psychological effects of digital media, he argues that the online social self (who people think you are) directly contributes to forming self-conception (who you think you are), and self-conception shapes personal identities (who you are).[18] In my view, even without full anonymity, digital media still provides humans with freedom to express and shape themselves, because the online social self deeply impacts genuine personal identities. Floridi's argument rejects the simplified dichotomy that all digital communications in anonymity are genuine and all online interactions in non- or partial anonymity are inauthentic.

Building on this discussion, I argue that digital anonymity can be a great benefit for people under considerable social and cultural pressures, as it allows them to communicate openly. At the same time, I acknowledge that digital communications that are not anonymous or are only partially anonymous can also allow digital media users in different contexts to practice authentic and genuine communications. The most critical point is that both positions reveal that digital media—the internet—significantly impacts communication patterns of people through the trait of open or authentic communication.

One limitation of this argument is that it does not answer the question of how digital communication patterns affected by the open communication available through digital media influence relationships between individuals.

17. Floridi, *Fourth Revolution*.
18. Floridi, *Fourth Revolution*, 64.

Digital Communication Patterns and Relationships

A limitation of the discussion between Putnam and Turkle is that it only deals with communications in public online settings, such as in online forums. Their argument focuses on online platform users who interact with others through inauthentic identities and who lack in-person relationships. Putnam and Turkle do not investigate how the open communication trait of digital media affects one-on-one relationships between individuals who have already built certain levels of face-to-face friendship. In the case of digital communication among friends who have in-person relationships, technically, complete online anonymity is unfeasible because of the preexisting offline relationships. However, since their communications are not publicly visible, digital media still provides security and confidentiality.

Communication scholars Patti M. Valkenburg and Jochen Peter answer the question posed above through the concept of online self-disclosure. They emphasize the importance of self-disclosure for the enhancement of relationship quality.[19] The concept of self-disclosure means that you exhibit your vulnerabilities. However, it does not mean that in complete anonymity you reveal your deep issues and secrets to the public online. Instead, it means that you share these with your friends—whom you already know in person—via mostly one-on-one internet media.

This type of communication pattern does not require complete anonymity; instead, it is based on confidentiality in trustworthy relationships. Valkenburg and Peter argue that when adolescent users share their innermost issues and feelings with their friends through instant messengers and social media, the online self-disclosure results in higher-quality friendships.[20] When one reveals personal frustrations and agonies to someone on digital media, this creates a bond, because the act of sharing something sensitive exhibits deep trust in the listener. At the same time, when the listener shows that he or she reliably maintains confidentiality for a friend, it increases his or her credibility. Therefore, this act of online self-disclosure enhances the quality of relationships by building mutual trust.

Supporting my argument, scholars for media studies argue that online self-disclosure can increase intimacy and closeness in the same way that offline self-disclosure can.[21] This suggests that openness or self-disclosure is an essential factor in deepening relationships both online and offline. In a similar vein, this point implies that relationships enhanced by self-disclosure

---

19. Valkenburg and Peter, "Social Consequences of the Internet."
20. Valkenburg and Peter, "Social Consequences of the Internet," 3.
21. Clark-Gordon et al. "Anonymity and Online Self-Disclosure."

Part One: Communication Patterns and Social Dynamics

may offer Adventist workers opportunities to engage in deeper, spirituality-related communication with their non-Christian young adult friends.

The trait of open communication affects communication patterns, and those digital communication patterns contribute to relationship development among Christian workers and their non-Christian young adult friends. For example, digital media may provide non-Christians with security and confidentiality, and those factors catalyze online open communication by encouraging non-Christians to share with their Christian friends their innermost thoughts, questions, and feelings. This act of online self-disclosure or openness has the potential to help foster deeper trust for spiritual dialogue. In this vein, through the field research, I sought to discover how digital media catalyzes open communication, including spiritual interactions, specifically between Adventist workers and their non-Christian young adult friends. I also sought to learn how digital media facilitates a deepening of relationships of trust and dialogue. I discuss the field research and my findings in chapters 4 and 5.

Second Trait: Connectivity by Mobile Communication

The second trait of digital media is connectivity. Richard Seyler Ling and Jonathan Donner, leading scholars on the impact of mobile phones, argue convincingly that the most significant impact of mobile communication is connectivity based on individual addressability, which means that all individuals became addressable and connectable due to their mobile communication devices, including smartphones.[22] Manuel Castells et al. assert that mobile communication's trait of connectivity has empowered youth culture: it increases autonomy by providing more peer-to-peer networking.[23] For example, according to Castells et al., safe autonomy depends on ubiquitous connectivity: individuals are able to become independent when they are addressable and connectable without being dependent upon a specific place or a group.[24] People who use digital mobile devices do not need to stay home to receive phone calls from their friends, because they can interact with their friends on digital media devices regardless of time and space.

This also means that the autonomy that comes as a result of the connectivity of digital media may allow digital media users to determine

---

22. Ling and Donner, *Mobile Communication*, 134–35.
23. Castells et al., *Mobile Communication and Society*, 245–55.
24. Castells et al., *Mobile Communication and Society*, 245.

their communication partners and topics. Since this connectivity enables people to interact with others regardless of time, space, and social circumstances, digital media users may choose friends and subjects who may be considered undesirable by other community members. For example, if they communicate on digital media, non-Christian young adults do not need to reveal their communication with Christian friends to their spouses or parents. This implies that the connectivity-based digital autonomy may allow non-Christians to participate in spiritual interactions with Christians without fear of judgment or reprisal.

This ubiquitous and continuous connectivity of digital media shows that the media enables humans to connect and communicate with others regardless of the barriers of time, space, and social situations. This point raises the question of how these omnipresent and continual digital communications affect relationships among individuals. To answer this question, I pay attention to the possibility that this continual connectivity may form a sense of connectedness among individuals. For example, when you frequently check in on your friends through digital media, they may experience that as care for their well-being. Likewise, if your friends feel that they may connect with you at any time through digital media, it can form—or increase—a feeling of connectedness or togetherness.

In line with my reasoning, communication and media scholars Darl Kolb, Greg Prussia, and Joline Francoeur argue that leaders' digital communication in conjunction with face-to-face communication is a critical element to establish and increase closeness, connectedness, or trust with peers and subordinates.[25] They go further by pointing out that digital connectivity enhances a sense of connectedness in face-to-face relationships.[26] This indicates that leaders' digital communication activities demonstrate their constant presence among their peers and subordinates, which contributes to forming a sense of closeness and connectedness that enhances the quality of relationships. For example, if employees notice that their leaders are continually available online for discussions and decision making, they feel that their leaders are constantly present.

This discussion demonstrates the possibility that the availability of connectivity through digital media can positively impact relationship development through continual connectedness and a pathway around the barriers of time, space, and social pressure. I thus anticipate that this digital

---

25. Kolb et al., "Connectivity and Leadership," 343–45.
26. Kolb et al., "Connectivity and Leadership," 349.

Part One: Communication Patterns and Social Dynamics

communication pattern can be an essential element of deepening relationships of trust and dialogue between Christian workers and non-Christian young adults. This point also indicates that a sense of closeness may lead Christians and non-Christians in MENA to communicate more deeply, which includes deeper spiritual interactions.

However, other scholars and researches argue that this level of connectivity has harmful effects on individuals' lives and relationships.[27] According to a study from Pew Research, even before the COVID-19 pandemic, 71 percent of parents in the United States expressed concerns about the destructive effects of smartphones on young children.[28] In a similar vein, research from the Barna Group describes how mobile devices interrupt sleep. For example, 82 percent of parents of teens confirm that their children bring smartphones to bed, and 62 percent of parents say that the first thing their children do in the morning is check their phones.[29] Turkle contends that this continual connectivity of digital media does not allow us to pay full attention to others in communications, and this distraction results in shallow relationships.[30] People are able to connect with everybody, but they may focus on nobody due to this over-connectivity of digital media. Because digital media allows you to be continuously available for everybody, while you exchange instant text messages with one friend, you may have to answer another friend's text. This dynamic may hinder the quality of relationships a person is able to maintain.

Douglas Rushkoff, the media theorist who coined such terms as *digital native* and *viral media*, reflects on the tendency of ruthless mobile communication:

> We work against the powerful bias of a timeless technology, and create a situation in which it is impossible to keep up. And so we sacrifice the thoughtfulness and deliberateness our digital media once offered for the false goal of immediacy—as if we really can exist in a state of perpetual standby.[31]

Rushkoff's point reveals two important implications of over-connectedness for relationships: First, a sense of constant connectivity via digital media

---

27. Auxier et al., "Parenting Children in the Age of Screens"; Crouch, *Tech-Wise Family*; Dyer, *From the Garden*; Rushkoff, *Program or Be Programmed*; Turkle, *Alone Together*.
28. Auxier et al., "Parenting Children in the Age of Screens."
29. Crouch, *Tech-Wise Family*, 90.
30. Turkle, *Alone Together*, 758.
31. Rushkoff, *Program or Be Programmed*, 29.

can bring about exhaustion. For example, people can feel pressure to be responsive and communicative regardless of their time and space. Even after work hours, employees may still need to communicate with their colleagues and supervisors through digital mobile devices. Christian workers may feel that they are obliged to interact with their non-Christian young adult friends during rest times because their digital mobile devices do not leave their hands. Earlier, I mentioned Turkle's assertion that digital media can cause distraction; the weariness caused by over-connectedness can cause a similar issue. Exhaustion may hinder deeply focused communication, which can limit the establishment of quality relationships.

Impetuous communication that is neither thoughtful nor deliberate is another issue. As Rushkoff explains, the connectivity of digital media enables users to respond promptly to communication, regardless of time and space. People do not need to take time to write and post their responses to friends and family anymore. You are always connected with everyone by digital media, and you can instantly act and react. This rapid digital communication style can bring about misunderstandings, because users tend to skip the deliberation required when responding to sensitive topics. Such misunderstanding can harm established relationships.

The relentlessness of digital communication that nudges people to be connected all the time may interrupt Christian workers' relationship development with their non-Christian friends. However, if this negative side effect can be mitigated, the sense of connectedness can be critical for building and nurturing relationships as well as for initiating spiritual interactions in the mission field. I thus argue that the connectivity of digital communication has the potential to foster relationships of trust and dialogue through a sense of continual connectedness, overcoming the barriers of time and space. This raises questions as to whether the technology may enable our frontline workers to form a sense of connectedness with non-Christian young adults regardless of time and space, and if so, how can workers avoid the downsides of connectivity? My field research and a pilot project explored these questions further. I discuss these later in this dissertation.

Third Trait: Interplay Between Real Life and Social Network Sites

The third sociality-related trait of digital media is its interplay with real life. According to danah boyd,[32] a technology and social media scholar

---

32. For personal and political reasons, danah boyd chooses not to capitalize her name.

Part One: Communication Patterns and Social Dynamics

who is a partner researcher at Microsoft Research, digital media—particularly social media—equates with real life and is critical for certain aspects of social life, such as maintaining and developing friendships.[33] This statement points out one important possibility for the connection between digital communication patterns and relationships: interplay between online and real-life communications may result in new ways of developing relationships. For example, established in-person relationships may catalyze digital communications among individuals when they exchange social media accounts, and those virtual interactions can help them further develop their real-life relationships by enabling them to learn about each other much more quickly than they would without digital media. Supporting this point, Floridi underscores the fact that digital communication technology has changed the way people begin, develop, and end their relationships with others.[34] In line with boyd and Floridi, theologian Angela Gorrell states that the value of relationship building is one of digital technology's glorious possibilities for young people: "Youth have a way of 'socializing' technology—that is, always finding a way of using technology to nurture relationships with their friends."[35]

However, several scholars assert that digital media's impact of interplay with real life is limited to the maintenance of preexisting offline relationships.[36] For instance, after graduation, alumni move their connections from offline college interactions to social networking sites. They do so in order to maintain their relationships and to support one another by sharing tangible opportunities, such as job openings.[37]

One issue is that an emphasis on the maintenance of preexisting offline relationships through the use of social media can be interpreted as an indication that social network sites are mere copies of real-life relationships. The claim limits the impact of digital media's trait of interplay with real life by reducing it to mere maintenance of preexisting offline relations, not recognizing its impact in deepening relationships of trust and dialogue. Some scholars disagree with this limited view based on the hybrid nature of online and offline communications. Sociologists Simon Lindgren and Michael

---

33. boyd, "Friendship," 79, 113.
34. boyd, "Friendship," 62.
35. Gorrell, *Always On*, 22.
36. Ellison et al., "Benefits of Facebook 'Friends'"; Goriunova and Bernardi, "Social Network Sites."
37. Ellison et al., "Benefits of Facebook 'Friends,'" 1164.

Dahlberg-Grundberg and ethnologist Anna Johansson explain the hybridity of digital media as "the coming together of online and offline, media and matter, or, more dynamically, as the interplay between the online and offline dimension."[38] Their argument reveals that digital media dynamically interacts with real-world relationships, and that interaction can result in deepening rather than simply maintaining relationships.

For example, scholars of psychology, counseling, and social work demonstrate a real example of how the hybridity between digital and offline communications can develop relationships. When mentors and youth communicate directly with one another on a daily basis through digital media, a sense of connectedness among them is increased.[39] Although the mentors and youth have preexisting offline relationships, when they also continue to communicate on digital media, it increases a sense of togetherness.[40] If people communicate with their offline friends through social media and instant messenger, this can foster a feeling of connectedness that advances their real-life relationships. Then the enhanced real-life relationships and interactions can catalyze deeper online communications—including spiritually or religiously sensitive interactions—that feed back to the offline friendships and communications. This means that hybrid online and offline communications have the potential to deepen relationships. Based on this discussion, I argue that digital media does not only maintain preexisting offline relationships but also enhances relationships through its interplay with real-life relationships.

This discussion suggests two important points for my research. First, digital media can be more effective for Christian workers to nurture relationships with MENA young people when they have preexisting offline relationships. Second, deepening relationships of trust and dialogue may be a result of fostering a sense of connectedness through digital media that leads Christian workers and non-Christians to spiritual interactions. These points reveal the significant relationship between digital communication patterns and deepening relationships of trust and dialogue, which corresponds to my central research issue. I examine these points further in chapters 4 and 5, where I discuss my field research.

---

38. Lindgren et al., "Hybrid Media Culture," 2.
39. Schwartz et al., "Mentoring in the Digital Age," 206.
40. Schwartz et al., "Mentoring in the Digital Age," 206.

Part One: Communication Patterns and Social Dynamics

SUMMARY

In summary, as a socializing technology, digital media has three sociality-related traits: open communication, connectivity, and interplay with real life. Those traits possibly relate to communication patterns that catalyze relationship development. In my view, digital media has significantly impacted communication patterns and relationship dynamics among individuals. The three traits of digital media can create a sense of continual connectedness among individuals, and that feeling of connectedness may deepen relationships of trust and dialogue that can create pathways for spiritual interactions between Christians and non-Christians.

I anticipated that the field research would allow me to observe the ways in which digital technology influences communication patterns, thus impacting the deepening of relationships of trust and dialogue among Adventist workers and non-Christian young adults. (I discuss the field research in detail in part II.) However, digital technology cannot be the only factor to impact relationships. Social dynamics, such as attitudes and values of Arab youth, as well as general trust-building factors, can impact relationship development. I thus review those aspects in the next chapter.

2

Social Dynamics and Relationships

IN THE PREVIOUS CHAPTER, I argued how digital media has impacted the ways in which people communicate and develop relationships. Spanish sociologist Manuel Castells's argument that digital media, such as the internet, shapes and forms social activities supports my position.[1] However, at the same time, Castells asserts that the media is not the sole factor determining social behaviors, because other elements, such as attitudes and values, can impact social interactions.[2] In addition, a part of the central research issue of this study is how social dynamics among Adventist workers impact relationships of trust and dialogue. I thus pay particular attention to the impact of social dynamics such as attitudes, values, and trust-building factors on relationship development among individuals.

To this end, my argument will be developed in two stages. First, I review the attitudes and values of the younger generation in the post-Arab Spring and how those attitudes and values potentially relate to relationship development. Because the goal of this study is to impact the deepening of relationships of trust and dialogue among Adventist workers and non-Christian young adults, I next scrutinize trust-building factors. This investigation will provide foundational knowledge for my central research issue and inform me about the data I need to obtain from the field research.

---

1. Castells, *Internet Galaxy*, 3.
2. Castells, *Networks of Outrage and Hope*, 106, 108.

Part One: Communication Patterns and Social Dynamics

THE POST-ARAB SPRING YOUTH: ATTITUDES AND VALUES

Young people in MENA have been neglected by social scientists as subjects of research for a long period, because Arab societies have not recognized this group. For example, Middle Eastern societies do not have a category for adolescents and young adults, despite the fact that these stages are ones of critical life transitions. These societies have traditionally identified only children and adults.[3] Since the early 2000s, young people in this region have begun to actively express their feelings and views through mobilizations and digital media. Because of this, the group has drawn recent attention from scholars, commentators, and research institutions. Moreover, the Arab Spring gave young people more visibility than ever before. Some scholars and research institutions have thus attempted to identify representative themes or pain points of the entire Arab youth in the post-Arab Spring context as a starting point for understanding their overarching attitudes and values.

The post-Arab Spring context for young people has been unstable politically and economically. Two significant keywords that represent the post-Arab Spring situation that young people in this region face are (1) uncertainty, or insecurity, and (2) anxiety.[4] Arabic studies scholar Jörg Gertel explains that the sources of the uncertainty experienced by young people are lack of control over the future and the current insecurities caused by political turbulence, economic downturn, and violence.[5] In a similar vein, in its 2016 Arab Human Development Report, the United Nations Development Programme (UNDP) describes young people in this region as enormously anxious about their future due to the insecurity of their circumstances.[6] Supporting UNDP, Ipsos, a market research company, defines the younger generation in the region as an anxious generation distressed by high prices, unemployment, corruption, violence, and moral decay.[7]

The issues of uncertainty and anxiety contributed to the emergence of two central attitudes of young people in the Middle East and North Africa

---

3. Gertel, "Uncertainty," loc. 312.

4. Ipsos, "MENA's Millennials Decoded"; United Nations Development Programme, "Arab Human Development Report 2016"; Gertel, "Uncertainty"; Gertel, "Youth in the MENA Region."

5. Gertel, "Uncertainty," loc. 601, 1209.

6. United Nations Development Programme, "Arab Human Development Report 2016," 17.

7. Ipsos, "MENA's Millennials Decoded," 18–19.

Social Dynamics and Relationships

(MENA): (1) desire for personal success, and (2) desire for trustworthy relationships.[8] Although the authors suggest other factors that influenced the two critical attitudes—for example, globalization, identity fragments, digital network, and violence—they present uncertainty and anxiety as the major premise of the discussion.[9] In light of the Arab Spring and the post-Arab Spring context, uncertainty and anxiety are the outcomes of political and economic instabilities. Based on this context, Jörg Gertel and David Kreuer identify community, success, freedom, and decency as four overriding values of MENA youth.[10] However, in my view, since the desire for personal success and trustworthy relationships expresses several points in the four values, I focus on discussing the two critical attitudes.

According to my interactions with the younger generation in this region, the desire for personal success displays young people's deep distrust of established systems, such as their governments. Throughout the period, the younger generation experienced these institutions' failure to provide securities for their lives. Governments and education could not guarantee job security or incomes sufficient to sustain their families, even after the Arab Spring. Beverley Milton-Edwards, a scholar for Middle Eastern politics, concurs with this point. In her research on Jordan in the post-Arab Spring period, she explains that the youth have become doubtful about the political, economic, and public systems of the country due to the unstable circumstances of the period.[11] For the same reason, even youth who uphold the authoritarian social structure desire the collapse of the impractical social system.[12] This demonstrates that the youth became distrustful when they observed that the established systems and authorities could not provide basic needs for them. As a result, rather than relying on institutions and systems, young people focus on individual efforts that provide materials, power, and influence.

This individualistic approach for success encourages young people in MENA to pursue their own agendas and make decisions according to emotions and interests, regardless of others' thoughts and views.[13] Because young people want autonomy to make their own decisions based on their

---

8. Gertel and Kreuer, "Values," loc. 1624.
9. Gertel and Kreuer, "Values," loc. 1249.
10. Gertel and Kreuer, "Values," loc. 1444–74.
11. Milton-Edwards, *Marginalized Youth*, 5.
12. Milton-Edwards, *Marginalized Youth*, 9.
13. Gertel and Kreuer, "Values," loc. 1454.

Part One: Communication Patterns and Social Dynamics

own perspectives, and because they want freedom to agree and disagree with others freely, the pursuit of personal success includes a pursuit of autonomy and freedom of expression. For example, Arab youth perceive religion as a personal issue.[14] This suggests that religion is no longer a group ideology that Arab youth have to uphold but is instead a personal matter that the younger generation can choose how to interpret and practice.

In my view, this discussion indicates the possibility that Arab youth may want to practice autonomy more than the older generation in the region do, and this value may have enabled them to interact with outsiders regardless of social, cultural, and religious boundaries. The youth are willing to decide who will become their friends, based on their personal interests rather than on cultural or societal expectations. This greater sense of autonomy among Arab youth implies that non-Christian young adults may be open to spiritual interactions with Adventist workers if they perceive that they and the workers share common interests. Further, this indicates that for the younger generation in MENA, common interests can be more important than common ideology.

Another key attitude of MENA youth as they respond to uncertainty and anxiety is a desire for trustworthy relationships. They long for trustworthy friends who value and embrace them, and such relationships require recognition, support, and the vulnerability of sharing innermost feelings and secrets.[15] These relationships built on trust can provide the youth with emotional and psychological security that traditional political and social systems cannot. This indicates a few critical elements of trustworthy relationships. First, trustworthy relationships require gestures of appreciation. When friends mutually recognize each other's friendships through words and actions, it may contribute to cultivating trustworthy relationships. In MENA, articulating positive emotions such as gratitude for companionship is an honorable action. In that sense, one's appreciation for friendship can be expressed candidly, verbally or online, and this can be a symbol of trustworthy relationships. Second, trust is often built on a foundation of clear demonstrations of support and care. This foundation may catalyze trust and build deeper relationships when individuals in difficult situations feel that their friends support and care for them. Finally, relationships built on trust entail deeper connections that allow individuals to safely share their opinions, doubts, painful feelings, and ideas with their friends. This implies

---

14. Ouaissa, "Religion," loc. 1937.
15. Gertel and Kreuer, "Values," loc. 1444.

Social Dynamics and Relationships

that Christian workers may build solid relationships and encourage open dialogue—including dialogue on spiritual topics—when they demonstrate appreciation and supportive care for their non-Christian friends. This shows that they are trustworthy friends with whom non-Christian young adults can share their innermost thoughts and emotions.

However, Christoph Schwarz argues that general values for the post-Arab Spring Arab youth need to be interpreted through the lens of the culture of the region. As an illustration, the author examines the value of autonomy. Although the rise of individualism and a desire for autonomy are primary themes in the post-Arab Spring, this does not mean that Arab youth want to practice complete self-determination apart from their families, because the family is still one of the most important institutions for MENA young people—both socioeconomically and emotionally.[16] Even across different groups in MENA, family is the society to which young people are most attached. However, young people desire to exercise moderate autonomy when making important decisions in their lives, such as the choosing of a spouse.[17]

Schwarz's argument reveals that the impact of social dynamics on relationship development among our workers and their young adult friends needs to be examined specifically in each context. I briefly examined general attitudes and values that may influence relationship development among young adults in MENA; however, this investigation does not reflect all nuances of the specific contexts of Adventist workers' youth ministries. Though the literature describes general attitudes and values of Arab youth as a part of social dynamics, the field research I describe later in this paper delves deeper into specific Arab contexts in which Adventist workers minister.

In the next section, I further explore general trust-building factors that can increase the quality of relationships and interactions. By investigating general factors of trust building, I hope to discover how trust can be formed in order to deepen relationships and interactions among individuals. This provides the theoretical foundations for my field research on relationship-building processes and spiritual interactions between Adventist workers and their non-Christian friends.

---

16. Schwarz, "Family and the Future," loc. 2554.
17. Schwarz, "Family and the Future," loc. 2393.

Part One: Communication Patterns and Social Dynamics

TRUST-BUILDING FACTORS

Trust can be a measure of depth of relationship. Edgar Schein's four levels of relationship theory show how trust relates to the depth of relationships among humans.[18] Schein categorizes human relationships into four levels: -1, 1, 2, and 3:

- *Level -1*: A level -1 relationship denotes no relationship or a negative relationship involving exploitation, such as between victims and criminals or slaves and slavers. Individuals in this group cannot expect any level of trust or authenticity as they interact with each other.
- *Level 1*: People who have level 1 relationships acknowledge one another, but they do not have personal friendships. The individuals who exist at this level of relationship include those such as professional service providers or seatmates on planes. The author asserts that people in this group demonstrate trust and openness to a certain extent while maintaining polite distance.
- *Level 2*: A level 2 relationship is one in which individuals relate to each other, but without intimacy, as their relationships have developed for common work, goals, or agreement. In this sense, individuals in this group have deeper trust and openness than do people in level 1, but the trust they have in one another is almost exclusively trust in the other not to harm them within their working relationships.
- *Level 3*: This is the most ideal human relationship, according to Schein. These relationships are those of close friendships in which there are love and intimacy. Trust in level 3 is deeper than in level 2, which means people in this group are willing to take risks to support one another and be vulnerable with each other.[19]

As this theory of four levels of relationship demonstrates, depth of trust affects how we measure the deepness of relationships, or vice versa. In this vein, trust and relationship are closely linked. This allows me to infer that a result of deeper relationships is the building of greater trust, which indicates a significant point for my study: if one can build trust, then one can have more open conversations about faith, and in these conversations, a trustworthy person's words will be given more weight. Therefore, trust

---

18. Schein, *Organizational Culture*.
19. Schein, *Organizational Culture*, 81.

Social Dynamics and Relationships

may allow for a place of safety where spiritual messages can be heard and considered by non-Christian young adults.

Several scholars for management, leadership, and organization support my point through their arguments that deeper trust in professional relationships can increase the quality of these relationships, which results in better work performance, more loyalty, and better behavior of both employees and customers.[20] Although my study does not deal with deepening trust in relationships for organizations, management, or business, these scholars' findings that trust can be a critical factor in interpersonal interactions as well as an indicator of deep relationships has implications for Adventist workers who wish to cultivate a higher receptivity to Christians and Christian messages. In this regard, the literature provides significant knowledge of trust-building factors among individuals. In addition, an understanding of general trust-building factors may enable me to discover how those social dynamics affect relationship development and spiritual interactions between Christian workers and non-Christian young adults.

Moreover, in the previous section, I explained that one key attitude of Arab youth in the post-Arab Spring period is a desire for trustworthy relationships that will help them deal with pervasive issues of uncertainty and anxiety. Although I briefly touched on the importance of trustworthiness for Arab youth and the relationship between trust and supportive care, I did not evaluate trust-building factors in general. I thus investigate what factors contribute to developing trust and how those factors work together in the process of building trust. I observed trust factors and indicators in relationship-building processes among Adventist workers and their non-Christian young adult friends during the field research, which I discuss in chapters 4 and 5.

Attributional Factors

Attributional factors refer to character traits of trustees that play critical roles in building trust with trusters. In the context of organizational settings, Kurt Dirks argues about the significant impact of leaders' characters and behaviors on their followers. Dirks explains that if followers notice

---

20. Dirks, "Three Fundamental Questions"; Doney and Cannon, "Examination of the Nature of Trust"; Laeequddin et al. "Trust Building"; Lewicki and Bunker, "Trust in Relationships"; Mayer et al., "Integrative Model of Organizational Trust"; McKnight and Chervany, "Reflections"; Moysidou and Hausberg, "In Crowdfunding We Trust"; Paparoidamis et al., "Role of Supplier Performance."

leaders' desirable traits, such as integrity, capability and compassion, they are more willing to reveal vulnerabilities to their leaders, because the leaders are perceived to be trustworthy.[21] Although this argument is not based upon an examination of personal relationships, it still shows the importance of a trustee's attributional factors.

The first attributional factor is integrity. If an employee needs to confidentially share a problem with an employer, knowing whether or not the leader is reliable and can maintain confidentiality can be critical. If an employee does not perceive that a superior possesses the trait of integrity, that person is far less likely to share confidential information with his or her leader. In this sense, integrity is equated with a trustee's authenticity or openness.

The second attributional factor is capability. Capability also plays a critical role in trust-building processes. When employees consider sharing problems with an employer, they may expect useful advice or solutions. If followers do not perceive that their leaders are capable of solving sensitive issues or even providing practical advice, they may not want to share such problems with their leaders.

Compassion is the third attributional factor. Leaders who demonstrate genuine care inspire their followers to be open with them. Ellen Whitener et al. explain benevolence as a demonstration of concern about the wellbeing of others or a willingness to improve the welfare of other parties.[22] If someone is experiencing delicate problems, that person will want to know whether or not a leader will respond to the issue with sympathy and kindness. If a follower perceives a leader's character to be indifferent, the follower will not want to share about any sensitive problems.

In my view, these attributional factors of trust building are also valid for personal relationships. People may only want to share their secret problems with friends who are perceived as honest, wise, and kind, because these individuals can keep secrets, provide useful and genuine advice, and demonstrate care about their friends' troubles. I argue that whether personal or organizational, characteristics of trustees encourage trusters to take risks. Roger Mayer, James Davis, and F. David Schoorman support my view, explaining that followers are more comfortable sharing sensitive information with leaders who are perceived to have those three character traits.[23]

21. Dirks, "Three Fundamental Questions," 17.
22. Whitener, "Managers as Initiators of Trust," 523.
23. Mayer et al., "Integrative Model of Organizational Trust," 715.

When trusters observe integrity, ability, and benevolence in trustees, they are more likely to take the risk of displaying vulnerability.

However, these factors and behaviors should be consistent. People need to experience these behavioral factors continuously in order to trust another. Whitener et al. suggest that behaviors such as demonstrating concern and behaving with integrity need to be consistent in order to build trust.[24] If trustees exhibit such behaviors randomly or inconsistently, trusters do not perceive them as reliable or predictable. Further, if these behaviors are unpredictable, trusters may not recognize them as genuine. Julian Rotter supports my view by arguing that interpersonal trust is defined as "an expectancy held by an individual or a group that the word, promise, verbal or written statement of another individual or group can be relied upon."[25] This means that when trusters perceive trustees' positive traits and behaviors as reliable and predictable, the depth of trust can be increased.

This discussion reveals two important points for my study. First, integrity, benevolence, and capability of trustees can enhance trustworthiness, which impacts depth of trust and relationships. This indicates the possibility that some of these factors may deepen trust and spiritual dialogue among Christian workers and their non-Christian young adult friends, thereby deepening relationships. It is important to note that trustees' attributional factors must be demonstrated consistently in order to deepen relationships. If these factors are unpredictable or inconsistent, trusters will not perceive them as authentic behavioral factors and, therefore, will fail to build trust or deepen relationships.

Cognitive Factors

While trusters can perceive trustees' attributional factors through repeated experiences in relationships, cognitive factors contribute to building trust when both parties have inadequate experience with each other. D. Harrison McKnight and Norman Chervany suggest that cognitive processes such as reputation inference, in-group categorization, and stereotyping impact initial trust.[26] Reputation inference means that one assumes positive characteristics of someone based on their connections to others.[27] For example, although one cannot know the character of a

---

24. Whitener et al., "Managers as Initiators of Trust," 523.
25. Rotter, "New Scale," 651.
26. McKnight and Chervany, "Reflections," 31.
27. McKnight and Chervany, "Reflections," 31.

person whom he or she just encountered, if a close friend introduces the unknown person as kind and honest, the secondhand information can allow for a certain level of initial trust.

Sherrie Komiak and Izak Benbasat refer to this type of information-based trust as "cognitive trust," which they define as a truster's "rational expectations that a trustee will have the necessary attributes to be relied upon."[28] This demonstrates that even when individuals do not have direct experience with one another, initial trust can be formed through rational evaluation based on reliable secondhand information. In this case, the most important factor for cognitive trust based on secondhand information is the reliability of the person who provides a truster with positive information about a trustee. In line with my view, Krystallia Moysidou and Piet Hausberg emphasize the importance of quality of information, stating that this is critical in order to establish cognitive trust when a truster does not have adequate experience with trustees.[29] This shows the potential of reputation inference to establish initial trust in new relationships. When one friend tells another about the positive characteristics of a new acquaintance, the quality of information can be increased based on the credibility of the recommender. Subsequently, the quality of this information enables the truster to make a sound judgment about how much initial trust to extend. This means that reputation inference can shorten the process of relationship development by providing an initial baseline of trust for both parties.

This theory of reputation inference reveals a critical point for my research: In the beginning of the relationship-building process, a friend's introduction can be an important factor in building initial relationships between Christian workers and non-Christian young adults. Even though the non-Christian young adults may not know about the characteristics of Christian workers, they may enter a relationship-building process if the Christian workers are introduced to the young adults by other friends. The role of these connections in relationship-building processes in MENA was examined through the field research, which I discuss in part II.

In-group categorization is another important cognitive factor for building trust. In-group categorization means that trusters categorize trustees as being part of their own group.[30] Like reference inference, in-group categorization allows trusters to build initial trust. This point raises

---

28. Komiak and Benbasat, "Effects of Personalization," 943.
29. Moysidou and Hausberg, "In Crowdfunding We Trust," 520–21.
30. McKnight and Chervany, "Reflections," 31.

a question about trusters' criteria for perceiving a trustee to be in the same group as them. Debra Meyerson et al. answer this question by suggesting that common denominators such as a common purpose and a joint task can create swift trust among parties without sufficient interactions or experience with each other.[31] This shows that joining a group in which the members share common interests, goals, and projects can be helpful for building initial trust, because those common denominators enable both parties to relate to each other. In line with this view, Ilhem Allagui argues that expressing common interests is important specifically for developing relationships with Arab youth.[32] Because of this, I argue that in-group categorization through the sharing of common interests and the pursuit of a mutual purpose may enable individuals to nurture relationships through a sense of kinship that builds initial trust. For example, if one encounters a person who would like to learn the same foreign language, that factor can catalyze their interactions through relevant talking points. These interactions that occur when individuals share common interests can result in a sense of connection that contributes to building trust.

This theory of in-group categorization reveals a vital point for my research: The initial trust that exists when individuals belong to the same affinity group can be beneficial for Christian workers who desire to build relationships with non-Christians who share their interests and goals. These affinity groups can be in such places as schools or social clubs, because members of those groups share mutual interests and a purpose. In the field research of this study, I, too, found that affinity groups were important for building relationships. Later in this dissertation, I describe specific ways in which group affinity was a useful tool in developing trust between Christian workers and MENA youth in their relationship-building processes.

Risk Factors

One may misunderstand the term *risk factors* as obstacles that hinder the process of building trust. However, the meaning of risk factors in relation to trust is positive rather than negative. Several scholars examine the relationship between risk and trust building. Niklas Luhmann defines trust as "an attitude that allows for risk-taking decisions."[33] One example of this kind of risk-taking is that once trust is established between individuals, they tend

---

31. Meyerson et al, "Swift Trust and Temporary Groups."
32. Allagui, "Changing Nature of Socialization," 47.
33. Luhmann, "Familiarity, Confidence, Trust," 98.

to expose their weaknesses to other parties because they rely on the other's discretion. In this sense, Denise Rousseau et al. argue that "willingness to be vulnerable" is a vital element of trust.[34] Both Luhmann and Rousseau et al. suggest that risk-taking is both an indicator and a result of trust.

However, other scholars argue that risk can also be an antecedent factor for building trust. Trust cannot exist if everything is secure and certain, because emergence of trust entails uncertainty.[35] For example, when trusters reveal their vulnerabilities, they take the risk of exposing secrets to other parties. In this sense, individuals need uncertainty and environments in which they can assume risk. Rajeev Bhattacharya et al. make the point that trust requires risky situations. In line with this view, Alex Michalos explains that uncertain circumstances allow trusters to display their trust in an optimistic future.[36]

To sum up, risk is both an antecedent factor and a result of trust. Uncertain environments provide trusters with opportunities to assume risk, and when they experience positive outcomes as a result of assuming risk, it enhances trust between individuals.[37] Risk is an indispensable element of building trust, and both risk and trust are interconnected in the process of deepening relationships.

This theory of risk factors demonstrates an important point for my research: When a non-Christian young adult takes a risk and is vulnerable with a Christian worker, this can be a significant indicator of trust that can lead both parties to spiritual interactions. For example, it is a vital indicator of deep trust and a strong relationship when someone shares his or her problems with another, and the resultant vulnerability can open a door to spiritual interactions. I sought to verify these points through the field research, which I discuss in part II.

Truster-Centered Versus Trustee-Centered

One crucial argument around trust factors is whether trust is embedded in trusters or trustees. This argument relates to whether deepening relationships of trust and dialogue among individuals depends on the trusters or trustees.

34. Rousseau et al., "Not So Different After All," 394.

35. Bhattacharya et al, "Formal Model of Trust Based on Outcomes"; Dasgupta, "Trust as a Commodity."

36. Michalos, *Good Policies and Business Ethics*.

37. Laeequddin et al., "Trust Building in Supply Chain Partners," 554.

Social Dynamics and Relationships

McKnight and Chervany explain that trust is a combination of trusting belief and trusting intention. Trusting belief refers to a truster's confidence in a trustee's attributional factors, such as capability, benevolence, and integrity. Trusting intention is a truster's willingness to depend on trustees.[38] In other words, to build trust, trusters need to believe that trustees are honest, competent, and compassionate, and they must be willing to rely on trustees.

Focusing on trusting belief, Rotter argues that trust is rooted in trusters, because if trusters are not convinced about trustees' positive attributional factors, trust cannot be formed.[39] This position points out that trust can be built according to trusters' emotional and cognitive judgments on trustees' characteristics and behaviors. In line with this, Patricia Doney and Joseph Cannon argue that trust entails the truster's evaluation of the integrity and benevolence of trustees.[40] According to Rotter and Doney and Cannon, trusters actively lead the trust-building process by judging trustees.

However, other scholars argue that trust is embedded in trustees, because without trustees' favorable characteristics, trusters cannot drive the trust-building process and assume risk. In this sense, Rousseau et al. value trustees' capability more than trusters' belief.[41] In a similar vein, Elena Delgado-Ballester, Jose Munuera-Alemán, and María Yagüe-Guillén argue that the trustworthiness of trustees' favorable characteristics enables trusters to build trust with other parties even in uncertain circumstances.[42] Although these scholars do not reject trusters' beliefs and intentions as critical components, they consider trustees' positive attributes and behaviors to be the starting points of building trust.

In my view, both positions—whether truster or trustee-centered—indicate essential elements of trust building. Even though trusters are the ones who decide whether they trust other parties or not, trustees' efforts to make themselves trustworthy are critical to enable trusters to believe trustees and to assume risk in uncertain situations.[43] This point demonstrates that trust building is a collective activity among trusters and trustees based

---

38. McKnight and Chervany, "Reflections on an Initial Trust-Building Model," 30.
39. Rotter, "New Scale."
40. Doney and Cannon, "Examination of the Nature of Trust."
41. Rousseau et al., "Not So Different After All."
42. Delgado-Ballester et al., "Development and Validation."
43. Laeequddin et al., "Trust Building in Supply Chain Partners," 560.

Part One: Communication Patterns and Social Dynamics

on mutual respect. The process requires both parties' desirable attributes and actions. For example, when trustees display integrity, benevolence, and capability, trusters respond to them by confidently taking risks. Therefore, I argue that trust is rooted in both trusters and trustees.

This discussion reveals one important point for my research: In line with what Schein says, if depth of trust equates with depth of relationship, I infer that the deepening of relationships is a collective activity that takes place between Christian workers and their non-Christian friends. This means that the process cannot be unilateral. Further, deepening relationships based on trust and dialogue requires bilateral communications and actions.

The literature would have been more useful to my research if it had included trust-building factors for Arab youth in a missional and interpersonal context. This limitation reveals the necessity to better understand the social dynamics through field research, focusing on relationship-building among Adventist workers and their non-Christian young adult friends. Building on this discussion, I argue that the gaps in the literature indicate the need for field research with a specific people group: Adventist workers and their non-Christian young adult friends.

SUMMARY

In this chapter, I first investigated the attitudes and values of Arab youth. Two keywords that describe the circumstances of the post-Arab Spring context are *uncertainty* and *anxiety*. In response to these issues of uncertainty and anxiety, Arab youth desire personal success because it provides materialistic security. This individualistic approach means that they seek autonomy to make their own decisions and freedom to express their thoughts, feelings, and ideas for pursuing their own agendas. The implication of this is that young Arabs may be more open than the older generation to spiritual interactions with Christians.

The second key attitude through which Arab youth deal with uncertainty and anxiety is a desire for trustworthy relationships that provide emotional security. Arab youth seek friends who recognize and support them, and they seek friends whom they can trust. In this chapter, I demonstrated that appreciation and supportive care are two central elements for building trust with Arab youth in order to open the door to spiritual interactions. Based on my examination of the values of Arab youth, I suggested several possibilities for communication patterns and relationships.

Social Dynamics and Relationships

Next, I discussed trust-building factors that can impact deepening relationships, such as attributional factors, cognitive factors, and risk factors. First, I argued that consistent characteristics and behaviors of trustees such as integrity, benevolence, and capability can positively impact the depth of relationships and communications. Second, I examined how secondhand information about trustees from credible sources and the sharing of common interests and goals can contribute to building initial trust, even without adequate experience and interactions among individuals. Third, I discussed how risks and uncertainty can be both the results and ingredients of trust building. Finally, I argued that like trust building, deepening relationships is a collective activity among individuals based on mutual respect, communication, and actions.

Although I identified the younger generation's attitudes and values in the post-Arab Spring through the literature and I examined general trust-building factors, those discussions do not provide me with sufficient knowledge about social dynamics that impact relationship-building among Adventist workers and their young adult friends in MENA. I thus emphasize the necessity of field research before the establishment of digital media model practices for Adventist workers.

Part Two

Field Research

A RESEARCH METHODOLOGY IMPACTS findings and allows other researchers to replicate the study. At the same time, it enables researchers to be on track during the study process.

In part II, I explain the three phases of exploratory sequential mixed methods I used and why I chose them for my field research. I then demonstrate the research process, including rationales, gaps, samples, and data collection. I also describe weaknesses and strengths of each method and how I endeavored to mitigate the limitations of the methods. I then share the data analysis method and key findings that emerged.

Through these descriptions, readers can understand both the big and small picture of this study. Finally, I discuss findings in the light of the literature review and implications of the findings for application.

3

Field Research Methods

I USED SEVERAL METHODS in pursuit of robust data regarding communication patterns among Adventist frontline workers and their non-Christian young adult friends in ministry, focusing on the relationship-building process involving digital media and social dynamics. Since the focus of communication patterns and social dynamics is Adventist workers' experiences of using digital media in their relationship building with young non-Christians in the Middle East and North Africa (MENA), I investigated their digital media practices by employing field research methodology. In this chapter, I look at the research rationale, sample selection, data collection methods, limitations, and the steps I took to secure validity and reliability.

RESEARCH RATIONALE

My literature review provided a rationale for field research. Below, I explain the need for field research by addressing gaps in the literature and field research questions.

Gaps Being Addressed

In the literature review, I focused on how communication patterns and social dynamics interact with human relationships. I looked at literature about the impact of digital media on relationships, focusing on the sociality-related traits of digital media. I also examined MENA youth's attitudes in the current post-Arab Spring period as well as general trust-building factors.

Part Two: Field Research

The gaps I discovered in the literature necessitate field research for the purposes of this study. For example, although the literature implies that digital media may play critical roles in the relationship-building process and spiritual interactions among individuals, it does not address Adventist gospel workers' experiences of using digital media in their relationship building—including spiritual interactions—with their non-Christian young adult friends. Thus, in order to discover how digital media affects Adventist frontline workers' relationship-building processes with non-Christian young adults, my field research focuses on the experiences of Adventist frontline workers using digital media in their relationship development and spiritual interactions with MENA young adults. With this intention in mind, in the next subsection, I present my field research questions.

Field Research Questions

1. What are Adventist frontline workers' young adult ministry practices for relationship building and spiritual interaction with young adults?

2. How is digital media impacting Adventist workers' young adult ministry practices?

3. What are the non-replaceable roles of in-person communication in Adventist workers' young adult ministry practices?

4. What roles has digital media played in the relationship building and spiritual interaction of young adult Adventist Muslim-background believers (MBBs)?

THE SAMPLE

I employed semi-structured interviews, a focus group, and a survey for this study. I conducted semi-structured interviews with forty Adventist workers, and I facilitated a focus group discussion with five young adult Adventist MBBs between the ages of twenty and thirty-eight. I then administered a survey with fifty-one Adventist frontline workers. The overall objective was to investigate the ways in which Adventist frontline workers' experiences of using digital media in relationship development with MENA young adults impact deepening relationship of trust among them.

Semi-structured Interview Sample

I conducted semi-structured interviews with forty Adventist frontline workers. These on-the-ground gospel workers are leading ministry activities in MENA; they understand their local contexts and the young adults to whom they minister.

From 2012 to 2020, in annual trainings and retreats, I trained our frontline workers for media and communication. I also interviewed these frontline workers for organizational reports and promotional materials. In addition, as the regional director for communication and media ministry, I often provided them with consultations regarding media and communication issues. Over these seven years, I have developed relationships with these workers, and through personal interactions and participation in various committees, I have become aware of their field activities.

With these factors in mind, after obtaining permission from the president of the mission, I identified forty-five frontline workers for semi-structured interviews according to the following criteria:

1. Current or former employees of the Middle East and North Africa Union Mission of the Seventh-day Adventists (MENAUM)
2. Current employees in locations where there are Christian churches and Christians are allowed to worship
3. Former employees living in non-MENA countries, such as Germany and the United States
4. Currently using or have used digital media on a daily basis in mission fields
5. Currently interacting or have interacted in mission fields with non-Christian MENA young adults online, offline, or both

After identifying workers who fit the criteria, I reviewed the names of the participants with ministry and regional leaders in person or by phone. By doing this, I could avoid keeping unnecessary written records about the participants.

The number of interviewees was based on the number of on-the-ground workers involved in young adult ministry in the region. The mission had approximately sixty in-field workers, but only about forty-five of these were directly involved in young adult ministries. In addition, some workers were unable to participate in the interviews due to reasons such as language barriers or in-field circumstances. In light of these factors, I strove to recruit for interviews a maximum of forty workers who fit the above criteria.

In order to verbally ascertain whether or not a worker would consent to be interviewed, I contacted each prospective interview participant by phone. Following this, I sent prospective interview participants a letter designed both to invite them to participate and to obtain their consent. I sent the letter to the interview participants as an encrypted message or email. Willing participants could send me the signed and scanned letters or reply to the email or text message with an indication of consent.

Focus Group Sample

Based on the outcome of the semi-structured interviews with forty Adventist frontline workers, I facilitated a focus group with five Adventist MBBs on September 13, 2020. As I previously mentioned, understanding how MENA young adults respond to digital media is not the focus of this research. However, the involvement of this group allowed me to probe the frontline workers' descriptions from the semi-structured interviews. Adventist MBBs have a greater understanding of MENA young adults' cultures and attitudes, since they have non-Christian backgrounds. At the same time, as they are now Christians, it was easy for these focus group participants to understand questions from an Adventist investigator.

From 2012 to 2020, for the purpose of mission promotion, I gathered numerous stories and testimonies about Adventist MBBs. Over these seven years, through personal interactions and participation in various committees, I also became familiar with some of these individuals.

With these factors in mind, I identified five Adventist MBBs who fit the following criteria:

1. Between twenty and thirty-eight years old
2. Publicly belong to a church community
3. Do not hide their Christian faith from their families and friends
4. Are not threatened by others due to their Christian faith
5. Use digital media daily
6. Reside in locations where Adventist entities are recognized by the governments, or in non-MENA countries
7. Interact with Adventist frontline workers

Field Research Methods

After I identified individuals who met these criteria, I reviewed the names with ministry and regional leaders in person or by phone. By doing so, I could avoid keeping unnecessary written records about the participants.

In order to explain the study and verbally ascertain whether or not a MBB would consent to be interviewed, I contacted each prospective focus group participant by phone. Once the prospective participants verbally expressed their intentions to participate, when I scheduled interviews, I also sent a consent form by encrypted text message. I asked them to reply with a clear indication of consent, since email was not a usual communication platform for them.

The number of focus group participants is based on the current circumstances of the mission. Although the Seventh-day Adventist Church has worked in this region for more than one hundred years, the mission only turned its attention to non-Christian populations in 2012. For that reason, the mission had only about eight young Adventist MBBs at the time of the field research. Some of these individuals were unable to participate in the focus group due to language barriers or in-field circumstances. Because of this, I strove to recruit every Adventist MBB who fit the above criteria.

Survey

Based on the outcomes from the analyses of the interviews and focus group discussion, I developed a survey instrument (see appendix A). Then, from September 21 to 28, 2020, I conducted a survey with fifty-one Adventist frontline workers in order to confirm the previous data and discover additional insights into the research. The survey participants fit the following criteria:

1. Current or former employees of the Middle East and North Africa Union Mission of the Seventh-day Adventists
2. If a current employee, must work in locations where Christians are allowed to worship
3. If a former employee in the MENA region, must live in a non-MENA country

I did not limit this group by whether or not they use digital communication media, because participants who do not use digital media could provide reasons for why they do not. Also, I did not limit this group by whether or not they participated the previous interviews, because the interview participants could still provide numerical data and additional insights that they were not able to offer during the interviews. However, two out of fifty-one survey participants were not able to finish the survey fully because they responded that they had no young adult friends in the ministry circle. Those in high-risk countries—such as Yemen, Iran, Libya, Syria, and the Kingdom of Saudi Arabia—were excluded from this research. If the conditions become safe and the security issues can be managed, further research in these countries would expand our understanding of the potential impact of digital media on young adult ministry.

Prospective participants received a pre-survey information sheet that included the following: "If you would be willing to participate in this survey, please read the following information. When the survey arrives by email or messenger, you will be asked to consent to the survey as it is described below." Following this, the pre-survey information sheet explained the researcher, the risks, the right to refuse, and the purpose of the research. The information sheet also ensured confidentiality.

Participants did not need to respond before I sent them the online survey link. Instead of requiring a signed consent form from each survey participant, the first survey question asked the participants about their understanding of the research and determined their willingness to participate in the survey.

As I mentioned above, the mission had approximately sixty in-field workers. Since I did not limit the survey group by whether or not they use digital media, I strove to recruit as survey respondents every frontline worker who fits the above criteria.

METHODS

I utilized three phases of exploratory sequential mixed methods.[1] Figure 3.1 presents the sequence of the mixed methods. I began the first phase with two qualitative methods—semi-structured interviews and a focus group—in order to understand an overall picture of phenomena or experience.[2] For the second phase, I built a survey instrument to test the outcomes from the

---

1. Creswell and Creswell, *Research Design*, loc. 4782; Flick, *Managing Quality in Qualitative Research*, 94.

2. Leedy and Ormrod, *Practical Research*, 331.

previous qualitative methods.[3] Finally, in the third phase, I administered the survey.[4] I employed several approaches for this research.

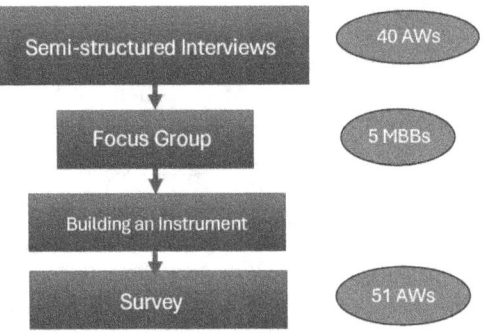

Figure 3.1: Conceptual Frame Flow Chart

Qualitative Approach

Although I have chosen to utilize the mixed methods of semi-structured interviews, a focus group, and a survey for phenomenological study, the primary methods are based on qualitative approaches. Edgar J. Elliston notes that qualitative research is placed at the center of missiological research, which deals with various aspects of "social, cultural, and/or spiritual life."[5] Qualitative research is used to investigate the world outside of laboratories and to comprehend and report social phenomena from insider perspectives.[6]

These indicate the legitimacy of utilizing qualitative methods as the foundation of my research design, which is intended to investigate Adventist frontline workers' experiences of using digital media in their relationship development and interactions with MENA young adults. This research project fits the criteria of missiological qualitative study as described above because it relates to the aspects of social, technocultural,[7] and spiritual lives

---

3. Creswell and Creswell, *Research Design*, loc. 4784.
4. Creswell and Creswell, *Research Design*, loc. 4784.
5. Elliston, *Introduction to Missiological Research*, loc. 350.
6. Kvale, *Doing Interviews*, loc. 121.
7. Philip Vannini, Jaigris Hodson, and April Vannini define *technoculture* as that "which refers simultaneously to the cultural dimensions of technology and to the technological dimensions of culture" ("Toward a Technography of Everyday Life," 463).

of Adventist frontline workers and MENA young adults. This also points to the suitability of a phenomenological approach for my research.

Phenomenological Approach

The philosophy of phenomenology was founded by Edmund Husserl (1859–1938), who demonstrated that the scientific method for physical phenomena is not suitable for scrutinizing human thought and action.[8] According to Daniel R. Shaw, "Missiological research is largely phenomenological" because it often concentrates on examining a specific people group.[9] However, investigating a people group or groups is not the sole purpose of a phenomenological approach.

Phenomenological approaches are used to understand people's common experiences, perceptions, feelings, and thoughts in specific contexts.[10] Rather than proving cause and effect, a phenomenological study describes what a people group or population experiences.[11] Since my research is aimed at describing Adventist frontline workers' experiences of using digital media in their relationship building and interactions with MENA young adults, a phenomenological approach is appropriate.

Mixed-Methods Approach

While the foundation of my research design includes the qualitative research methods of semi-structured interviews and a focus group, I also integrated the quantitative method of a survey into the qualitative research design. In recent decades, the demarcation between qualitative and quantitative approaches has become blurred; researchers now have more flexibility than before to utilize various methods.[12]

One potential benefit of using mixed methods is that qualitative and quantitative data can complement each other. Todd D. Jick explains, "Qualitative and quantitative methods should be viewed as complementary rather than as rival camps."[13] This statement implies that mixed

---

8. Husserl, *Essential Husserl*.

9. Shaw, "Qualitative Social Science Methods," loc. 3245.

10. Bernard, *Research Methods in Anthropology*, 23; Leedy and Ormrod, *Practical Research*, 273.

11. Bernard, *Research Methods in Anthropology*, 24.

12. Bernard, *Research Methods in Anthropology*, 298.

13. Jick, "Mixing Qualitative and Quantitative Methods," 602.

methods can contribute to increasing the validity of research findings by examining the consistency of the results from various methods.[14] For example, the validity of my research findings can be increased if semi-structured interviews, a focus group, and a survey produce the same results about Adventist frontline workers' experiences of using digital media in interactions with MENA young adults.

Another aspect of the complementarity between qualitative and quantitative methods is that they answer different types of inquiries. As I previously mentioned, qualitative data can explain experiences, feelings, thoughts, and opinions of a group or groups about phenomena, but they cannot answer questions of how much, how many, or how often.[15] For instance, while qualitative methods may describe the frontline workers' digitized interactions with young adults, these methods do not count how often workers use media to interact with young adults, nor do they track how many social media platforms workers utilize. A combination of qualitative and quantitative data can provide researchers with additional insights they would not be able to obtain from the qualitative or quantitative data alone.[16] For these reasons, I utilized mixed methods for this investigation.

DATA COLLECTION

As I mentioned above, I employed three methods for data collection: semi-structured interviews, a focus group, and a survey. In this subsection, I describe strengths and weaknesses of each method, including my efforts to alleviate the weaknesses. I then explain how I implemented each data collection method.

Semi-structured Interviews

Steinar Kvale recommends interviews as a powerful method for producing knowledge about human experiences, because "interviews allow the subjects to convey to others their situation from their own perspective and in their own words."[17] Interviews enable researchers to scrutinize the experiences, thoughts, and opinions of interviewees in order to understand a people

---

14. Bernard, *Research Methods in Anthropology*, 235.
15. Bernard, *Research Methods in Anthropology*, 385.
16. Creswell and Creswell, *Research Design*, loc. 501–4.
17. Kvale, *Doing Interviews*, loc. 425, 460.

group and phenomena from the interviewees' viewpoints.[18] According to Corrine Glesne, good interviews are similar to baseball: when interviewers pitch questions, interviewees hit them.[19] In the research interview, knowledge is discovered and established through the interaction between interviewers and interviewees.[20] These statements acknowledge that interviews are interactive activities rather than unilateral data-collection methods. This characteristic of the interview method provided opportunities to explore topics related to the central research issue of this study.

In addition, I chose the interview method not only to collect quality data but also to provide frontline workers with opportunities to voice their feelings and experiences. In the process, they communicated new ideas of what factors contribute to making effective use of digital media in deepening relationship of trust with young adults.

Semi-structured and unstructured interviews are the primary forms of qualitative interviews.[21] Although both methods allow for extensive interactions between interviewers and interviewees within a specific timeframe, I have chosen semi-structured interviews for reasons I address in the following subsection.

Strengths and Weaknesses

One of the benefits of the semi-structured interview method is that it offers a balanced combination of pliability, rigorous data, and effective time management. While semi-structured interviews give interviewers flexibility to acquire in-depth information, the method also enables researchers to use limited time effectively, according to interview guides. This increases the reliability of the data by ensuring the same questions are asked of all participants.[22]

I interviewed forty Adventist frontline workers. Given the number of interviewees and the limited time frame for data collection and analysis, conducting each interview without a segmented time or an interview guide could have been less effective. A strength of the semi-structured interview format is that it lends itself to effective time management. Semi-structured interviews help interviewers to stay within the boundaries of the topic,

18. Rubin and Rubin, *Qualitative Interviewing*, 3.
19. Glesne, *Becoming Qualitative Researchers*, 67.
20. Kvale, *Doing Interviews*, loc. 292.
21. Rubin and Rubin, *Qualitative Interviewing*, 31.
22. Bernard, *Research Methods in Anthropology*, 212.

while unstructured interviews often allow interviewers and interviewees to become distracted.[23] Since I focused on collecting data about how digital media has affected Adventist workers' in-field ministries with young adults, the semi-structured interview method was necessary to acquire relevant data from each interviewee within the one-hour time frame.

A common criticism of semi-structured interviews is that respondents might omit certain information or might not trust the interviewer, thus leading to flawed data.[24] This critique points out that the interviewees' lack of openness and trust can be an impediment to conducting quality semi-structured interviews.

In order to mitigate these issues, I used a twofold strategy: (1) create a comfortable interview atmosphere, and (2) ensure confidentiality. I endeavored to create a comfortable and relaxed interview mood to encourage frontline workers to voice their genuine thoughts and stories. In regard to this aspect, Clark Moustakas suggests, "Often the phenomenological interview begins with a social conversation or a brief meditative activity aimed at creating a relaxed and trusting atmosphere."[25] Taking this into account, I spent approximately five minutes on social conversation before beginning each interview.

IMPLEMENTATION

After I gained human subject research approval on June 16, 2020, I reviewed with ministry leaders the names of forty-five Adventist workers who met the previously described criteria. I then contacted each prospective interviewee by phone to explain about this study and interview process. When a prospective interviewee expressed willingness to participate, I then scheduled an interview and sent an informed consent letter. I prepared questions for semi-structured interviews before proceeding (see appendix A). Then, from June 26 to July 14, 2020, I conducted semi-structured interviews with forty Adventist frontline workers.

To interview Adventist frontline workers, I utilized the online communication platform Zoom for data collection. This circumvented any travel challenges due to COVID-19 and allowed for security and confidentiality. The mission has already employed such platforms to communicate with on-the-ground gospel workers, utilizing security practices such

---

23. Creswell, *Qualitative Inquiry and Research Design*, 43.
24. Glesne, *Becoming Qualitative Researchers*, 97.
25. Moustakas, *Phenomenological Research Methods*, 94.

as pseudonyms and coded words in communication. In addition, online interviews were preferable, since an on-site visit may interrupt frontline workers' ministry environments by drawing the community's attention. The average length of each interview session for Adventist frontline workers was about sixty minutes.

From these interviews, I was able to investigate the following: (1) frontline workers' ministry practices for relationship building and spiritual interactions with young adults, and (2) their experiences of using digital media both in relationship development and spiritual interaction in young adult ministries.

Focus Group

After I conducted semi-structured interviews and obtained in-depth information about frontline workers' experiences, I facilitated a focus group with five young Adventist MBBs I know personally. Since the focus of my research was on Adventist frontline workers, in the focus group I only touched lightly on the experiences of digital media among MENA youth. I limited this part of the research to this focus group of Adventist MBBs and not to a cross-section of MBBs in the region because (1) my focus was not on how MENA young adults respond to digital media, and (2) a foreign Christian researcher collecting data from a non-Christian population for ministry purposes could arouse suspicion and increase the risk for mission work in the region. Thus, I collected data from young Adventist MBBs who intimately understood non-Christian young adults' cultures and attitudes and could share information about what roles digital media has played in their own relationship building and interactions with Adventist workers. Data from these young adult participants strengthened my understanding of Adventist frontline workers' experiences of digital media in relationship development and interactions with young adults.

For this research, the focus group method was a group interview in which the interaction between researcher and participants was not the sole means of gathering data; the interaction among participants played a vital role. David L. Morgan articulates the core concept of focus groups: "The hallmark of focus groups is the explicit use of group interactions to produce data and insights that would be less accessible without the interaction found in a group."[26] In accordance with Morgan's notion of focus groups, I, as a

---

26. Morgan, *Focus Groups as Qualitative Research*, 2.

Field Research Methods

researcher, interacted with individuals in the focus group. In addition, I was also able to obtain through participant interaction relevant data about how digital media affected young Adventist MBBs' spiritual growth.

Strengths and Weaknesses

In comparison to individual interviews, one potential strength of focus groups is that the method enables researchers to investigate group interactions around a specific issue.[27] Morgan states,

> Group discussions provide direct evidence about similarities and differences in the participants' opinions and experiences as opposed to reaching such conclusions from post hoc analyses of separate statements from each interviewee.[28]

I observed similarities and differences in Adventist MBBs' opinions about Adventist frontline workers' experiences of digital media in interactions with MENA young adults. For example, while all the participants agreed about digital media's importance in their overall experience with Adventist workers, they gave different weights to its roles in relationship building and spiritual interaction. Some stated that digital media played a more critical role in relationship building than in spiritual interaction, while others expressed the opposite. Second, in terms of time management, focus groups are more efficient than individual interviews for data collection and analysis. Morgan argues that performing two eight-person focus groups are more time efficient than conducting ten interviews, because through group discussions the researchers can obtain data directly related to specific research inquiries within a limited time period.[29]

Finally, the focus group method can be used to supplement data from other previous methods.[30] Shaw explains that focus groups enable researchers to validate data;[31] through focus groups, the researcher can investigate responses from previous interviews or observation.[32] This points to my experience that the focus group with Adventist MBBs validated previous interviews with Adventist frontline workers.

27. Flick, *Designing Qualitative Research*, 85.
28. Morgan, *Focus Groups as Qualitative Research*, 10.
29. Morgan, *Focus Groups as Qualitative Research*, 13–14.
30. Morgan, *Focus Groups as Qualitative Research*, 2.
31. Shaw, "Qualitative Social Science Methods," loc. 3306.
32. Shaw, "Qualitative Social Science Methods," loc. 3309.

However, this strength directly relates to a primary weakness of focus groups. As researchers organize and moderate focus groups, their influence affects participants' interactions—hence, the accuracy of the data can be questioned.[33] Another limitation is that in focus groups, participants tend to agree outwardly with other participants and to withhold opinions they might express in private. At the same time, in focus groups, participants are inclined to demonstrate more radical perspectives than they would in private.[34] In order to alleviate these shortcomings of the focus group, I used three tactics: (1) promote freedom of expression, (2) create a comfortable discussion atmosphere, and (3) examine participants' responses against their contexts.

To these ends, I used encrypted online communication to ensure confidentiality within usually small Christian circles. I also assured participants that (1) none of the information will identify them by name, (2) all recorded data will be securely stored in an encrypted digital format, and (3) all audio files and notes will be destroyed upon completion of this research. In addition, before beginning the focus group recording, I used the first ten minutes of the focus group to introduce participants and create a relaxed atmosphere. Finally, my knowledge of the participants' circumstances and backgrounds helped me to examine and navigate their interactions.

IMPLEMENTATION

I focused on collecting data about what roles digital media has played in relationship building and spiritual interaction between MBBs and Adventist workers. Following the semi-structured interviews with forty Adventist workers—which took place from June 26 to July 14, 2020—and the data analysis process, I prepared questions based on the analyzed data for a focus group discussion (see appendix A). Then, on September 13, 2020, I conducted a focus group discussion with five Adventist MBBs between the ages of twenty and thirty-eight. For conducting the focus group, I utilized the online communication platform Zoom in order to maintain confidentiality. Although these MBBs publicly belong to Christian communities and reside in locations where Christians are allowed to worship, online communication was preferable in order to ensure confidentiality within small Christian circles. The length of the focus group discussion for Adventist MBBs was about ninety minutes.

33. Morgan, *Focus Groups as Qualitative Research*, 15.
34. Morgan, *Focus Groups as Qualitative Research*, 15–16.

I experienced two challenges with the focus group format. First, because of the different time zones in which the focus group participants reside as well as their individual schedule conflicts, scheduling the one-time focus group discussion took more than two weeks. Second, the participants tended to interact with me more than with their fellow participants. Because of this, I had to make sure to engage all of the participants and ask each of them his or her opinion. Despite these challenges, I was able to collect valuable data that confirms the Adventist workers' experiences.

Survey

Based on the outcomes of the interviews and focus group discussion, I conducted a survey of fifty-one Adventist frontline workers. The purpose of this was to confirm the data from the primary interviews and discover additional insights for application. The primary purpose of a survey is to produce a quantitative representation of data about a specific population; the primary method for data collection is asking the sampled participants a series of questions.[35] The process is to ask questions of respondents via prepared questionnaires, followed by a numerical analysis of their responses.[36]

Louis M. Rea and Richard A. Parker explain that surveys are being used broadly because various researchers and organizations understand that this method displays attitudes, perspectives, and opinions of sampled respondents.[37] Surveys enable researchers and organizations to generalize findings for a larger population in order to produce policies and improve services.[38] Since this research is intended to identify digital media model practices that deepen Adventist workers' relationships with young adults, surveying them is an appropriate method.

However, the method does not stand alone for this research. As I mentioned earlier, a survey can supplement previous data collected by qualitative methods, because while qualitative data answers inquiries about what and why, it cannot answer questions about how much and how often.[39] While semi-structured interviews and a focus group are useful to understand Adventist frontline workers' experiences, feelings, thoughts, and opinions of using digital media in their relationship building and

---

35. Fowler, *Survey Research Methods*, 1.
36. Leedy and Ormrod, *Practical Research*, 159.
37. Rea and Parker, *Designing and Conducting Research*, 4.
38. Creswell and Creswell, *Research Design*, loc. 3394–400.
39. Bernard, *Research Methods in Anthropology*, 385.

Part Two: Field Research

interactions with young adults, the survey can answer questions about how often the workers use digital media as well as the level of importance of media in their ministry environments. Thus, I employed a survey together with semi-structured interviews and a focus group.

Strengths and Weaknesses

Survey research benefits researchers and their studies in several ways. Survey research enables researchers to collect data quickly and efficiently in comparison with other methods, such as interviews and observation.[40] Through the current diffusion of online media, the method has become more feasible and efficient than before.[41]

Another advantage is that survey research can investigate a transient moment in time, similar to taking a quick photographic snapshot of an ongoing event.[42] Thus, given the time frame of data collection and rapidly changing digital media trends, together with other methods, a survey can be an effective means to understand frontline workers' experiences of using digital media in interactions with MENA young adults.

The survey method, however, also has disadvantages. While survey research is an efficient way to obtain data quickly, the method is limited in discovering the deep reasons behind the responses that respondents provide. In a similar vein, survey research does not collect data through mutual communication. Instead, the method instructs participants to provide answers without involving the researcher in a listening process.[43] In order to mitigate these weaknesses, first, I used a survey along with the qualitative methods of semi-structured interviews and a focus group. In doing so, I was able to obtain information from both qualitative and quantitative methods, as they supplemented each other.

Second, in order to avoid leading or coercing respondents to answer questions in specific ways, I provided respondents with various options for answers. For example, the participants were able to choose more than one answer to a single question. In addition, for each question, participants could add comments to clarify their choices or note that none of the options accurately reflected their experiences. In this way, participants could flexibly respond to questions.

40. Ruel et al., *Practice of Survey Research*, 30.
41. Ruel et al., *Practice of Survey Research*, 30.
42. Leedy and Ormrod, *Practical Research*, 159.
43. Leedy and Ormrod, *Practical Research*, 159.

IMPLEMENTATION

After the focus group discussion with five young Adventist MBBs on September 13, 2020, and the initial data analysis process, I prepared survey questions based on the analyzed data (see appendix A). In order to increase the response rate, the survey was designed to take approximately ten minutes to complete. I distributed a pre-survey information sheet through regional leaders to invite Adventist worker participation. I conducted the survey with fifty-one Adventist workers. For the survey, I employed the online survey platform Qualtrics, with password protection and the exclusion of an IP address tracking option. This means that only those who received a password via an encrypted message could participate in the survey.

LIMITATIONS

There are several limitations to my findings. First, although I strove to recruit participants who met the above criteria for interviews, a focus group, and a survey, readers need to limit generalizations, because the sample only reflects contextual and cultural values of the Seventh-day Adventist Church in the Middle East and North Africa. This means that generalizing from one set of results can be risky. For example, my findings may not be applicable for the entire Christian mission in the region. In addition, limited availability of young Adventist MBBs within the mission resulted in only five MBBs participating in the focus group. Therefore, generalizations based on the MBB focus group are limited.

Second, I endeavored to include Adventist workers who work in various countries within MENA for this project. However, my final participant selection does not evenly represent all the countries in which we minister. Each mission field in diverse countries and cities within MENA has different cultures, demographics, and languages. In addition, those in high-risk countries such as Yemen, Iran, Libya, Syria, and the Kingdom of Saudi Arabia were excluded from this research. These factors point to the limitation of generalization of my findings for all the mission fields within MENA.

Finally, my findings are possibly biased in favor of missional use of digital media, since I conducted this research with a missional intent as an Adventist Christian media professional. In next subsection, I explain my efforts to minimize these limitations by attempting to ensure validity and reliability.

Part Two: Field Research

VALIDITY AND RELIABILITY

The notion of objectivity is central to discussing validity and reliability for both qualitative and quantitative research methods, because objectivity of research can be measured and realized by reliability and validity.[44] For scientists, objectivity is critical, because objective, logical, and systematic methods for analyzing reality allow them to produce reliable knowledge.[45] In this sense, objectivity is vital for qualitative and quantitative researchers in order to create knowledge instead of mere opinions.

However, securing objectivity does not mean an absolute and permanent absence of bias. Jerome Kirk and Marc Miller refer to such a concept of objectivity as "a naive and inhumane version of vulgar positivism."[46] In a similar vein, H. Russell Bernard offers the following critique: "The idea of truly objective inquiry has long been understood to be a delusion."[47] Yet objectivity is still important for researchers, because if researchers do not strive to attain objectivity, they force readers to accept their subjective opinions.[48] Investigators need to be transparent about their research measurements and processes so readers and other researchers can detect the errors and biases. The highest degree of objectivity can be attained by ensuring as much validity and reliability as possible.[49]

Validity

Validity means the accuracy of methods, data, and findings in research.[50] For example, valid data can directly answer research inquiries, because it is useful, relevant, and accurate to solve research problems.[51] Hence, validity critically affects the credibility of the research.[52]

John Creswell and David Creswell suggest multiple approaches to increase the accuracy of findings. Triangulation is one method that many qualitative researchers use to obtain validity through collecting various

---

44. Kirk and Miller, *Reliability and Validity*, 20.
45. Lastrucci, *Scientific Approach*, 6.
46. Kirk and Miller, *Reliability and Validity*, 20.
47. Bernard, *Research Methods in Anthropology*, 5.
48. Kirk and Miller, *Reliability and Validity*, 20.
49. Kirk and Miller, *Reliability and Validity*, 20.
50. Bernard, *Research Methods in Anthropology*, 53.
51. Elliston, *Introduction to Missiological Research*, loc. 3058.
52. Creswell and Creswell, *Research Design*, loc. 4302–3.

Field Research Methods

forms of data.[53] If several methods yield the same results, the findings are more likely to be valid.[54] Following this notion of triangulation, I employed three methods: (1) semi-structured interviews, (2) a focus group, and (3) a survey. Data collected from frontline workers via semi-structured interviews was examined by a focus group of young Adventist MBBs and a survey of a larger group of Adventist workers.

Another approach is to disclose researchers' empirical, cultural, and philosophical biases and assumptions, because those factors affect researchers, their findings, and their interpretations of the data.[55] I thus strove to demonstrate my biases, assumptions, and background. For example, I explained that I conducted this research as a foreign Christian media professional for missional purposes. As a result, readers will take the context into account when they evaluate the findings and conclusions of this research. In a similar vein, presenting findings and themes that contradict the primary hypotheses and themes is critical, because validity can be increased by debating opposing information.[56] Therefore, I endeavored to be transparent in my presentation of findings and themes—negative or positive—in order to obtain validity of the research.

Reliability

Elliston defines reliability as "the degree of consistency of a research instrument or method."[57] Validity of a measurement instrument might be increased by improving its reliability, because "we can measure something accurately only when we can also measure it consistently."[58] Reliability depends on whether researchers are able to produce the same answers by a measurement procedure in different circumstances.[59] Bernard uses a thermometer metaphor to explain the notion of reliability:

> If you insert a thermometer into boiling water at sea level, it should register 212 Fahrenheit each and every time. "Instruments" can be

---

53. Creswell and Creswell, *Research Design*, loc. 430810.
54. Bernard, *Research Methods in Anthropology*, 235.
55. Shaw, "Qualitative Social Science Methods," loc. 3254.
56. Creswell and Creswell, *Research Design*, loc. 4322–25.
57. Elliston, *Introduction to Missiological Research*, loc. 1757.
58. Leedy and Ormrod, *Practical Research*, 118.
59. Kirk and Miller, *Reliability and Validity*, 19.

Part Two: Field Research

things like thermometers and scales, or they can be questions that you ask people.[60]

Elliston suggests two approaches to increase reliability of interviews and focus groups. First, interviewers need to be consistent in how they ask questions—this includes facial expressions, tone, and wording. If each interviewee or group is asked questions in different ways, it can create different answers and decrease reliability.[61] Conversely, reliability may be increased when the interviewer asks multiple interviewees the same questions in the same way. Second, interviewers need to ask questions that interviewees can answer knowledgably.[62] If respondents are asked questions they cannot answer, researchers may not be able to obtain saturated data that has reached the point when no new information can be discovered.

Given these suggestions, I strove to utilize detailed research procedures, including protocols for semi-structured interviews and a focus group. In doing so, I could repeat the same questions consistently in order to increase reliability. In addition, I pretested the semi-structured interview and focus group method in order to ensure that respondents understood the questions. In the next subsection, I discuss validity and reliability of the survey method.

Validity and Reliability of Survey

One potential challenge to the validity of a survey is whether or not respondents answer honestly.[63] Often, the investigator's presence constrains the respondents' answers.[64] In order to diminish this issue and increase the validity of survey research, I used a web-based survey with password protection and the exclusion of IP address tracking. In addition, via a pre-survey sheet, I informed all the participants that the online survey does not collect identifying information and that their responses will remain anonymous.

However, due to the lack of the investigator's involvement, this strategy introduces a reliability issue for the web-based survey. When respondents do not understand a question or when the scope of a question is limited,

---

60. Bernard, *Research Methods in Anthropology*, 54.
61. Elliston, *Introduction to Missiological Research*, loc. 1816.
62. Elliston, *Introduction to Missiological Research*, loc. 1816.
63. Punch, *Survey Research the Basics*, 42.
64. Rea and Parker, *Designing and Conducting*, 23.

there is no one present to explain.[65] In order to avoid this issue, I pretested the survey and adjusted the questions for better understanding. At the same time, I designed multiple-choice questions that allowed respondents to choose more than one answer. I also included a comment box for each question to allow respondents to write in other answers. I utilized these strategies and approaches to increase validity and reliability of the research.

SUMMARY

Utilizing the mixed methods of semi-structured interviews, a focus group, and a survey based on a phenomenological approach was suitable for my research. These approaches enabled me to engage with Adventist workers and Adventist MBBs, and it allowed them to express their thoughts and share their experiences. Through this process, I obtained data I then analyzed to ascertain communication patterns and social dynamics affecting Adventist workers' relationship development with non-Christian young adults.

I endeavored to mitigate the weaknesses of each data collection method, and I took steps to increase the degree of validity and reliability for this research through a triangulated methodological approach. Because of this, I have confidence that the data is reliable and valid. As the process unfolded, I observed the data's consistency between different methods and the logical relationships between themes. With this in mind, I now turn to my findings.

---

65. Rea and Parker, *Designing and Conducting*, 13.

4

Findings: Impact of Digital Media on Relationship Building

To IDENTIFY DIGITAL MEDIA model practices that can deepen Adventist workers' relationships with non-Christian young adults, it is essential to understand Adventist frontline workers' perceptions, evaluations, and usages of digital media; their experiences of relationship building and interaction with young adults in the Middle East and North Africa (MENA); and their potential needs in their ministry contexts.

In order to understand Adventist workers' experiences of using digital media in their relationship building and interactions with MENA young adults, I conducted interviews, a focus group, and a survey. In this chapter, I display key findings from my research process. This chapter is divided into two sections. First, I describe my process of data analysis. Second, I underline the themes that emerged from the data about the impact of digital media on relationship-building processes among Adventist workers and non-Christian young adults.

DATA ANALYSIS

I used Creswell's data analysis spiral to analyze the data for this research (see figure 4.1). This spiral consists of five basic phases: (1) managing and organizing data, (2) reading and memoing emergent ideas, (3) identifying and classifying themes, (4) developing and assessing interpretations, and

Findings: Impact of Digital Media on Relationship Building

(5) representing and visualizing the data.[1] According to this data analysis spiral, I moved through the following steps for data analysis:

1. *Managing and organizing data.* I arranged the collected data by creating a file-naming system and then transcribing the audio recordings of the interviews and focus group. I then imported the transcripts to the coding application Dedoose.

2. *Reading and memoing emergent ideas.* I perused the data in order to obtain a general picture. During this phase, I employed the critical strategy of writing my thoughts and impressions about noticeable information.[2]

3. *Identifying and classifying themes.* Using the coding application Dedoose, I described and classified themes from the data. While I read the data, I formed codes by combining the text into small categories of information. Then, through reviewing and re-reviewing, I reduced these into twelve themes.[3]

4. *Developing and assessing interpretations.* I evaluated codes, categories, patterns, and themes I created during analysis for applicability to my research. I then organized these into larger units of abstractions.[4]

5. *Representing and visualizing the data.* In this final phase of the spiral, I presented the data with tables, figures, and text. By reviewing the research questions and data, I decided what formats—such as quotations and coding table—work best.[5]

---

1. Creswell and Poth, *Qualitative Inquiry and Research Design*, 317; Leedy and Ormrod, *Practical Research*, 315.
2. Gibbs, *Analyzing Qualitative Data*, 24.
3. Creswell and Poth, *Qualitative Inquiry and Research Design*, 410.
4. Creswell and Poth, *Qualitative Inquiry and Research Design*, 419.
5. Creswell and Poth, *Qualitative Inquiry and Research Design*, 422.

Part Two: Field Research

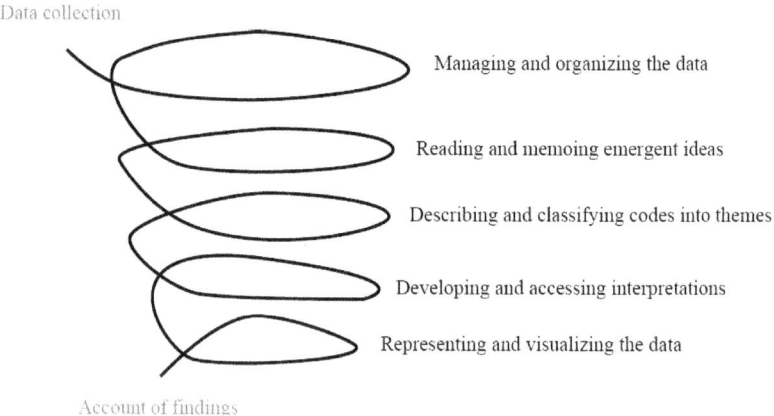

Figure 4.1: Creswell's Data Analysis Spiral[6]

KEY THEMES

The central research issue of this study is to explore how communication patterns and social dynamics among Adventist workers and young adults in MENA impact deepening relationships of trust and dialogue. In this research project, the term *communication patterns* primarily indicates ways in which Adventist workers and non-Christian young adults interact and exchange information with each other through digital media for relationship building and interaction. In consideration of the communication nature of the media, I use *digital communication media* (*DCM*) interchangeably with *digital media*. *Social dynamics* indicates relationships and interactions;[7] therefore, in this research, the term refers to Adventist workers' relationship building and spiritual interactions.

My four field research questions (summarized in table 4.1) are designed to investigate the central research issue. The first research question (RQ1) investigates Adventist workers' young adult ministry practices, mainly exploring relationship building and spiritual interactions among Adventist workers and non-Christian young adults. The second question (RQ2) examines the impact of digital media on young adult ministry practices, surveying Adventist workers' perceptions, evaluations, and usages of digital media in order to understand this method of communication with

---

6. Creswell and Poth, *Qualitative Inquiry and Research Design*, 317.
7. Farmer et al., "Social Dynamics Management," 3.

young adults. The third field research question (RQ3) scrutinizes the role of in-person communication among Adventist workers and young adults in order to understand the full picture of communication patterns. The fourth question (RQ4) explores the social dynamics and communication patterns among Adventist workers and young adults from the perspective of Adventist Muslim-background believers (MBBs). In the focus group, I asked for the MBBs' opinions about Adventist workers' previous answers for RQ1, 2, and 3. Therefore, in the following subsections, I look at RQ4 alongside the other three field research questions.

Table 4.1: Field Research Questions and Categories

RQ	Topic	Variables	Participants
RQ1	Relationships Spiritual interactions	Social dynamics	AWs
RQ2	Digital communication media	Communication patterns Social dynamics	AWs
RQ3	In-person communication	Communication patterns	AWs
RQ4	Probing RQ1–3 by young MBBs	Social dynamics Communication patterns	MBBs

After interviewing forty Adventist workers, facilitating a focus group with five MBBs, and administering a survey with fifty-one Adventist workers (see appendix B), I found eleven key themes in response to those four field research questions.

Relationship-Building Process

The first field research question asked the following: "What are Adventist frontline workers' young adult ministry practices for relationship building and spiritual interaction?" Relationship development is a vital part of young adult ministry practices and social dynamics among Adventist workers and young adults, as explained above. In order to answer this first question, I examined key themes of the relationship-building process among Adventist workers and non-Christian young adults. I then explored

Part Two: Field Research

how digital media relates to this process and the impact of digital media on the relationship-building practices. Table 4.2 presents the three themes that emerged in the category of the relationship-building process. The total number of interviewees includes those who participated in the semi-structured interviews. I also included codes with a lower number of mentions in the interviews if they received a high number of responses in the survey results or if they indicated noteworthy findings.

Table 4.2: Relationship-Building Process

Category	Theme	Code	Total Number of Interviewees
Relationship-building process	Started through spontaneous contact	Affinity connection	30
		Friend connection	18
		Online	3
	Maintained by mingling	Desire for social interactions	34
	Deepened by trust	Care	31
		Openness and genuineness	20
		Exemplary life	18

STARTED THROUGH SPONTANEOUS CONTACT

Many Adventist frontline workers mentioned that spontaneous in-person encounters were their first connections with young adults in MENA. Thirty out of forty interviewees answered that their initial encounters with their young adult friends were unexpected and spontaneous (see table 4.2). Of the survey participants, thirty-seven responded that spontaneous in-person encounters are how they first encountered their young adult friends (see Q8 in appendix C). However, during the analysis process, I observed that although Adventist workers and young adults met for the first time by accident, that spontaneous in-person encounter occurred as a result of common language studies or university affiliations, shared affinities for

Findings: Impact of Digital Media on Relationship Building

sports, or other common interests. I thus coded spontaneous in-person encounters as "affinity connections."

A language school is a common place for Adventist workers to meet their young adult friends, because language acquisition is usually the first step for workers when they arrive in their fields. One male worker noted that a language school "has been a very good place to encounter local young adult friends" (AW-19).[8] A local university is another place where Adventist workers initially encounter young adults. One female worker explained that a university provides diverse opportunities to meet young non-Christian friends (AW-34). Another male worker remarked, "Almost 100 percent of my non-Christian friends I met at the university" (AW-25).

Social activities and sports also provide Adventist workers with opportunities to connect with young adults. One male worker described how sports provided him with the most constant and frequent opportunities to engage with young adult friends. He remarked, "There is a group for running, and I met approximately 50 percent of my non-Christian young adult friends through running" (AW-44).

Young adults' various individual interests often lead them to Adventist workers. One frontline worker was alone at a church playing the guitar, and the church door was open. A young non-Christian passed by the building. Drawn by the guitar playing, he walked into the church and sat down to listen. According to the worker, "He asked me, 'Oh, you play the guitar?' Then we became friends" (AW-31).

Often, Adventist workers are introduced to young adults by other friends, and such connections expand frontline workers' relationships with young non-Christians. Eighteen Adventist workers stated that they were introduced to their young adult friends by others (see table 4.2). In addition, thirty-three of the survey respondents chose the connection through friends as the first connection opportunity (see Q8 in appendix C). One worker remarked on the relationship-expanding process: "A friend of mine introduced me to his friend, and then the new friend connected me to another friend. In this way, my relationship circle with young adults is getting bigger every year" (AW-38).

Overall, MENA young adults encountered Adventist workers most frequently through various affinity connections: language schools,

---

8. In order to preserve the anonymity of participants, I refer to each by a code rather than by name. AW refers to a frontline Adventist worker, and MBB refers to a Muslim-background believer. For a detailed list of interview dates and the corresponding coded participants, see appendix B.

universities, sports, mutual friends, and individual interests. Only ten survey participants responded that they first connected with their non-Christian friends through institutionally organized community events, such as cooking classes or health campaigns (see Q8 in appendix C).

One unexpected finding is that the use of digital media does not play a significant role in creating initial connections between Adventist workers and young adults. Only five survey participants responded that they made their first connections with young adults via DCM (see Q8 in appendix C), and only three semi-structured interviewees mentioned digital media as their initial means of connection with their young non-Christian friends (see table 4.2).

The above observation indicates the following: First, if on-the-ground workers have opportunities to encounter their young adult friends face-to-face, digital media may not be critical for first connections. However, this finding does not tell how digital media affects existing relationships. I investigate this further in the next section, where I report on DCM's impact on relationship building. Second, MENA young adults are open to relationships with non-Muslim outsiders if they share common interests, such as sports, health, languages, cultures, school activities, and hobbies. This also means that places and activities in which young people are often involved provide Adventist workers with opportunities to connect with MENA young adults.

Maintained by Mingling

Socializing is the way most Adventist workers maintain their relationships with young adults. Thirty-four interviewees mentioned that mingling with young adults was critical for maintaining relationships (see table 4.2). Of the survey respondents, thirty-seven workers answered that they could most easily maintain these relationships by meeting in cafés or restaurants, visiting their young adult friends in their homes, and participating in sports (see Q9 in appendix C).

One frontline worker reflected on the importance of sharing meals with his young adult friends. He observed, "In the Middle East, eating together is very essential to relationship" (AW-1). Another worker commented, "Discussing something with a cup of tea or playing a board game. That is how we maintain our friendship" (AW-40).

Findings: Impact of Digital Media on Relationship Building

Cafés and restaurants are not the only places for socializing or mingling. One female worker shared how she could maintain her relationships with friends by social interactions in the school. She explained,

> I have a lot of reasons to meet my classmates because we need to do homework and projects together. And so, like all the weeks through the school year, we are meeting a lot. And every day in the classroom, there is a reason to talk, to share, and everything. (AW-30)

Although those social activities seem to happen naturally, they are initiated by mutual desire for connection. One worker noted, "We try to spend a lot of time together. We go out, we eat, we attend parties" (AW-9). One young Adventist MBB's experience supports this: "We tried to meet as many as often as possible, like hanging out in a café, or having a sport activity" (MBB-50). In sum, Adventist workers maintain their relationships with young adults by mingling in various places. While this social interaction seems to be organic and natural, it requires a mutual desire to spend time together in a common activity.

DEEPENED BY TRUST

Adventist workers deepen their friendships with young adults by building trust. The workers mentioned three major factors for establishing deep trust: demonstrating care, openness, and an exemplary life. In the following, I describe how each factor contributes to building deep trust between Adventist workers and young adults.

CARE

According to interviewees, when MENA young adults experience the care of Adventist workers, they are better able to trust their Adventist friends. Of the fifty-one survey participants, forty-one workers responded that offering genuine care to young adult friends was critical to establishing deep trust (see Q11 in appendix C). Thirty-one out of forty interviewees mentioned care as the most important factor for building deep trust between Adventist workers and young adults (see table 4.2).

Several workers shared that expressing affection for their non-Christian young adult friends is critical in MENA culture. One male worker shared his observations about this:

> I know that—especially in this culture—like when someone's sick or someone has a crisis, if you visit them, or if you call them, that's something meaningful. If you don't come and check on them, or take them some food or something like that, you're showing that you don't care about them. Or just doing things that they find meaningful to show caring. (AW-5)

Gospel workers' willingness to help young adults when they have any problems displays Adventist workers' care for their non-Christian friends. One worker described how, through helping, he earned the trust of his university classmates: "In my class, if someone needs my help, I'm always there. So if someone asks me something, even if it's late or even if I am tired, I always try to do something. I say, 'Okay, let me help you. What do you need?'" (AW-28). Although both expressing affection and demonstrating a willingness to help seem to be obvious indications of care, I present them here to illustrate how DCM can be utilized to create a sense of care. This is one of the ways in which digital media plays a role in relationship building.

Being a safe person from whom to seek counsel is another critical element for building trust. One worker shared his story about how his young adult friends tested his trustworthiness:

> We assure our friends that whatever we share together, no other person will know about it. We always make sure that we don't tell any other family or any other person about what some of the families are facing or what they tell us. So one after another one, sometimes they tell you a very small secret, just to try if you will tell others. When they feel that you are a safe person, it builds up, and then the relationship will be stronger. (AW-15)

This implies that young adults experience care when their innermost feelings and frustration are heard and acknowledged. During the focus group discussion, one Adventist MBB shared about how comfortable she feels with her Adventist friends: "I feel that it is easier to share difficult issues with Adventist friends—more than with my brothers and sisters. I feel that we are really a family, even though we are from different countries. I can confidently say that there is no shame" (MBB-46). Other MBB participants agreed with this worker's experience: they became comfortable with their Adventist friends after they had experienced genuine care. Several other Adventist workers also mentioned that when their young adult friends come to them with personal issues, they understand that this is an indication of deep trust.

Findings: Impact of Digital Media on Relationship Building

Openness

Openness is the second vital factor for building deep trust. Twenty interviewees mentioned openness as a factor for establishing deep trust (see table 4.2). One female worker described how she gained trust by being open about herself: "When you are real, when you show the real you with your weaknesses and good things, the person trusts you because they feel that you don't hide like others" (AW-37).

This type of openness enables Adventist workers to accelerate the trust-building process. One worker observed,

> The deep trust comes when you are reciprocating what they are sharing. What I mean by that is that they're not just telling me their problems, I'm telling them mine. We've both got to be willing to be vulnerable, otherwise they're not going to really, truly be comfortable opening up to you. I have seen that relationships really grow much faster when I can really be open with them. (AW-8)

Similarly, one Adventist MBB described how genuine openness and care are important for building trustworthy relationships and spiritual interactions. He remarked, "I wanted to emphasize on the fact that the friendship should be genuine and authentic. When we really care for people, for who they are, so deep and big spiritual conversations will open up any time sooner or later" (MBB-51).

Exemplary Life

Several workers mentioned that they were able to gain deep trust from MENA young adults because of the presentation of their exemplary lives. Eighteen out of forty interviewees mentioned that their exemplary lives allowed them to build deep trust with their non-Christian friends (see table 4.2).

Young adults can begin to trust Adventist workers when they observe the attitudes and behaviors of Adventists that set them apart. One worker explained, "They see that you always speak good words without bad words and gossiping, respecting the others. So they see that you are different" (AW-4). Another worker observed that how Adventist workers treat others increases the trust young adults have in them. He shared his story:

> There was a wealthy landowner where we lived, and he would stand over his worker. He would just stand there over him, not

picking up anything. It immediately shows that he is a too valuable person to do work that would get him dirty or make him sweat. But with me, I hire someone to work for me, then I'm working alongside of them. It would help break down barriers, and people would tell me, "You're like one of us, you might have a car and drive it, but you are working your land with me, which is extremely unusual." (AW-3)

Not only are individual workers positive examples to MENA young adults, the families of Adventist workers can also serve in this way. One married worker described how his family life was influential in gaining trust and encouraging young adults to open their hearts:

> They perceive my family as a happy family. So many times they say, "Look, you have a perfect life. You have a nice family—you are happy. We don't have anything. Our country is a mess. Our family doesn't care about us. Our religious leaders don't care about us. There are no jobs for young people in this country." (AW-14)

The relationships between Adventist workers and young adults are maintained by mingling and are deepened by trust. When Adventist workers demonstrate care, openness, and exemplary lives, this helps to establish deep trust. Not surprisingly, DCM as a communication tool plays a role in relationship building. The following section traces how DCM functions as a tool for developing trust.

Impact of DCM on Relationship Building

The second field research question asks the following: "How is DCM impacting Adventist workers' young adult ministry practices?" In the following, I present key themes that emerged in my research regarding the impact of digital media on the relationship-building process among Adventist workers and young adults. Table 4.3 presents two themes in the category of impact of DCM on relationship building.

Findings: Impact of Digital Media on Relationship Building

Table 4.3: Impact of DCM on Relationship Building

Category	Theme	Code	Total Number of Interviewees
Impact of DCM on relationship building	Catalyze interactions	Getting to know each other	17
		Provide relevant talking points	15
		Promote open expressions	20
	Create a sense of togetherness and care	Checking on each other	31
		Overcoming the barriers of time and space	33

CATALYZES INTERACTIONS

Although digital media does not play a significant role in creating initial connection opportunities, it accelerates relationship development by catalyzing interactions. Of the interviewees, seventeen frontline workers mentioned that DCM provided Adventist workers and young adults with opportunities to learn about each other (see table 4.3).

Several Adventist workers explained that exchanging DCM contacts with young adults after the first in-person connection is common. One worker commented, "One of the first things they ask is my Instagram and Facebook [ID]. So immediately after we meet, they add me, or I add them, and then we start our communications" (AW-14). Another worker explained, "They ask my Instagram and Facebook ID even before my mobile number" (AW-18). For MENA young adults, asking for someone's DCM information at a first-time meeting is considered socially acceptable. One female worker explained,

> So here in this country, it's normal for them. If they just met you, they tell you, "Okay, give me your Messenger, give me your Facebook, give me your Instagram," because this is how they keep in touch with you. So I was so surprised because it's not usual in my culture to just, I meet you one day, five minutes ago, and then you

just ask me my Facebook or my Instagram. But here, it is really the way that they communicate. (AW-34)

Once Adventist workers and non-Christian young adults connect via digital media, they can learn about each other through digital interaction. One worker commented that, via DCM, "We can understand what they like to do, what they like to talk about, or how they like to express their feelings and thoughts. So this is the way it helps us to get closer and establish a stronger relationship" (AW-23). Another worker stated that although he would prefer in-person communication rather than digital communication, digital media accelerated his relationship-development process with young adults. He remarked, "I felt the need of seeing my friends and spending time together. Nevertheless, the fact is that [DCM] helped us a lot to build bridges that I think physically would have been longer" (AW-43).

Digital media also provides Adventist workers with relevant talking points for their communication with young adults. Fifteen out of forty interviewees mentioned that they were able to ascertain pertinent conversation topics through DCM (see table 4.3). Digital media allows Adventist workers to reach out to their non-Christian friends. One worker remarked, "Once, someone posted a picture of a crying woman on WhatsApp. I was able to have conversations about the status. I used it to start a new conversation" (AW-45). This implies that Adventist workers can learn about their non-Christian friends and discover relevant talking points when young adults express themselves on digital media.

In this vein, Adventist workers experienced young adults as more open and expressive online than in real life. Twenty out of forty interviewees mentioned that their young adult friends are more candid and communicative online than in person (see table 4.3). One worker commented, "Most of my friends behave more conservative and traditional in person than on DCM. When they use DCM, they open themselves in a way that they would never do in person" (AW-25). Another worker observed,

> My friends don't speak much about their ideas and how they view things in real life. But then when they go on social media, they start expressing their frustrations even with religion. They start expressing and sharing things that don't make sense in their views [on DCM]. (AW-16)

Findings: Impact of Digital Media on Relationship Building

One worker described the immediacy of digital media in young adults' revelations of negative life events and feelings, which contrasted with the slower pace of in-person communication:

> When I ask my friends about how they are doing, they simply say that they are doing okay. But on social media, they are sharing: "I'm sad because someone from my family is ill or died or in my university, something happened." So, on DCM, they express quickly and shortly what is going on. But when we are in a personal meeting, it takes long before they can feel comfortable to talk about some things. When they are on DCM, they are more open to express their feelings, their thoughts, how they understand the world. (AW-23)

Young adults also actively display their openness toward different cultures. One worker described,

> They pretty much like to be seen as open-minded in the sense that they absorb a lot of the influence from Western culture, and they like to make that public on DCM. So there are other people posting things related to sports or culture or music or pop culture in the West. (AW-14)

The above illustrations demonstrate that Adventist workers can quickly learn about their young adult friends on digital media because young adults are more open and expressive there. It also implies that on DCM they experience less pressure to conform to traditional cultures.

Digital communication plays an important role in how Adventist workers build relationships with young adults. DCM allows Adventist workers and young adults to quickly learn more about each other after a first-time meeting, and it provides Adventist workers with relevant topics for their communication with young adults. This relationship-building process on DCM happens quickly because young adults are able to express themselves more openly via media than they are in real life. Digital media thus accelerates the relationship-building process. One MBB commented, "We can save time [through DCM]. It is important because it creates the links, it gives the trust, and it gives time to build the friendship" (MBB-50).

CREATES A SENSE OF CARE AND TOGETHERNESS

Another finding in relation to the impact of DCM on relationship building among Adventist workers and young adults is that through digital media,

Part Two: Field Research

Adventist workers can extend care and nurture a sense of togetherness. I discovered two primary digital media functions that form and foster the feeling of togetherness and care: (1) checking on each other and (2) overcoming the barriers of time and space.

Checking on Each Other

Thirty-one interviewees mentioned that when they casually check on non-Christian young adult friends via digital media, these friends experience a sense that Adventist workers care about them (see table 4.3). One worker explained the significance her WhatsApp text messages have for her young adult friends: "Messages mean that you care about your friend" (AW-10). Another worker stated that when he checks on young adults through digital media, it demonstrates his friendship (AW-31).

Even short and casual communications can be meaningful. One worker noted, "They appreciate that a lot, because you remember them, so you send them a message, just saying, 'Hi!' or 'How are you?' They appreciate that" (AW-27). Another worker described how reaching out to his young adult friends via DCM is critical even if he encounters these friends in person every day. He remarked,

> I think it shows that people really care about you or you really care about people. I believe that it means a lot. In some other cultures, if your friend says, "Good morning," it is just a casual greeting without a significant meaning. But here, even if you see your friend every day in the morning, it is important for you to say, "How are you? How is your son? How's the family?" You will spend some time just on checking on your friend. I believe it's important for MENA young adults. (AW-1)

Another female worker shared a story about how receiving messages through digital media was meaningful to her refugee friends who experienced crises in their lives. She observed,

> And just to know that somebody cares about them, somebody's concerned about their well-being, checking to make sure they're, like, having food in their house or that their kids are all right even though they're not in school, that means a lot to families. So when we would check in with them, they . . . were really impressed that it wasn't just that we were concerned about their kids but that we were also concerned about the whole family. (AW-5)

Findings: Impact of Digital Media on Relationship Building

As I have illustrated, digital communication allows young adults to experience care from Adventist workers. This is true when Adventist workers inquire after MENA young adults, regardless of length or seriousness of messages. This implies that the sense of care young adults experience when they are checked on via DCM can contribute to establishing trust between Adventist workers and young adults, and that trust deepens relationships and spiritual interactions.

Overcoming Barriers of Time and Space

Another observation in relation to the second field research question is that DCM creates a sense of togetherness between Adventist workers and young adults by enabling them to overcome the barriers of time and space through constant digital communication. Thirty-three out of forty interviewees mentioned that DCM allows them constant communication with their young adult friends, regardless of time and location (see table 4.3).

One worker described the effectiveness of DCM for his relationship development with young adult friends:

> The best thing is that you can connect with people, even though they are not able to go out because it's late night or they have children. Yes. Mostly it's about the time and the space, I think, especially in my experience. (AW-39)

One worker commented, "The biggest thing of DCM is that it gives a feeling that I am always connected with my non-Christian friends" (AW-18). The feeling of connectedness through DCM strengthens the relationships among Adventist workers and MENA young adults. One worker shared, "We cannot maintain relationships if we don't send messages. When I send them a message, we keep our relationship" (AW-20).

In this context, digital communication increased workers' influence on their non-Christian friends by creating a sense of co-presence. One worker shared her experience about DCM: "You have an opportunity to enter that person's life that God can use, at any moment of the day. So it is just an amazing opportunity to have that instant connection. It's invaluable. The ministry of presence at any time is a huge blessing" (AW-2).

The sense of togetherness that is created by ubiquitous digital communication allows MENA young adults to experience care from Adventist workers. One worker commented, "I can keep in touch constantly with

Part Two: Field Research

that person, even when I am doing many things. It makes somebody feel that they're important and that I care about that person" (AW-31). One worker reflected on how such digital communication led to deeper friendships with young adults:

> [DCM] definitely creates a deeper friendship, because it shows that you're interested in the person's everyday life. We are always messaging each other; then when something bad happens, or something really good happens, they're automatically sharing those things with me. (AW-8)

In a similar vein, one MBB stated, "It is just very quick to send a message and ask for your prayer when we are in trouble. We have used that, and it was very useful" (MBB-49).

Another finding revealed through the interviews is that the sense of togetherness and care that DCM makes possible has become even more vital during the COVID-19 pandemic. Of the fifty-one survey respondents, twenty Adventist workers stated that the pandemic has moderately increased their use of DCM with young adults (see Q54 in appendix C), and seventeen Adventist workers responded that their use of DCM with young adults has markedly increased due to the pandemic (see Q54 in appendix C). Twenty-one interviewees also mentioned the pandemic when discussing how DCM contributes to an experience of care and togetherness. One worker commented, "[DCM] has shortened the distance, firstly. It has allowed us to be connected in this lockdown. I couldn't meet with my friends in person during the past four months" (AW-44).

In summary, although DCM does not play a critical role in creating the first connection between Adventist workers and young adults, it is vital in maintaining and strengthening relationships. Digital communication media is an extension of face-to-face relationships, so media contributes more to strengthening existing relationships than to creating new relationships. Forty-two out of fifty-one survey participants responded that maintaining and strengthening relationships with MENA young adults is the main value of using DCM in their young adult ministries (see Q28 in appendix C). Of the survey participants, twenty-four responded that DCM is very effective for relationship development with young adult friends, and ten respondents stated that it is extremely effective (see Q28 in appendix C).

As I illustrated in the previous subsection, expressions of care help Adventist workers to establish deep trust, and deepened trust opens the door for spiritual interaction. When Adventist workers check in via digital

Findings: Impact of Digital Media on Relationship Building

communication, it can allow MENA young adults to experience care and a sense of togetherness that transcends the barriers of time and space. Figure 4.2 illustrates the impact of DCM on the relationship-building process.

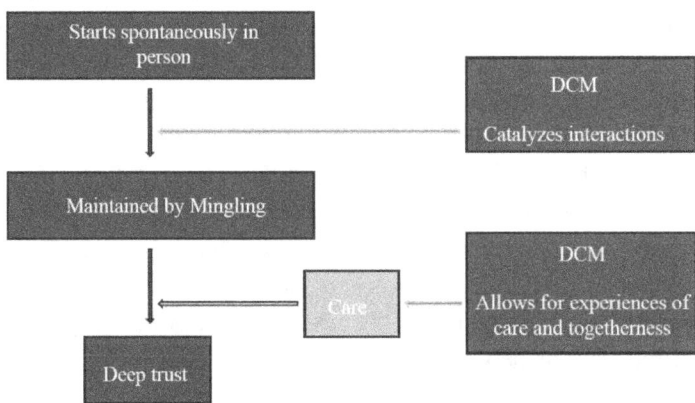

Figure 4.2: Impact of DCM on the Relationship-Building Process

SUMMARY

In this chapter, I presented key themes of Adventist workers' relationship-building process, which is part of their young adult ministry practices and social dynamics. Adventist workers encountered non-Christian young adults most frequently through different affinity connections: language schools, universities, sports, introductions by friends, social clubs, and day-to-day activities—digital communication media did not play a critical role in the first connection. Adventist workers obtain opportunities to connect with MENA young adults through places and activities in which young people are often involved. However, this does not express how digital media affects other aspects of relationship building. This needs to be investigated further. It is also vital to recognize that MENA young adults are open to relationships with non-Muslim outsiders if they share common interests, such as sports, health, languages, cultures, school activities, and hobbies.

DCM is the part of the communication patterns and social dynamics Adventist workers utilize to build relationships with MENA young adults. Thus, in this chapter, I presented how DCM relates to relationship building. DCM plays a significant role in maintaining and strengthening relationships among Adventist workers and young adults. First, DCM provides them with opportunities to learn about each other. Second, it enables Adventist workers to approach young adults with relevant topics. Finally, MENA young adults experience care when Adventist workers utilize DCM to regularly check in on their young adult connections, overcoming barriers of time and space. In addition, the importance of DCM for young adult ministry has increased during the COVID-19 pandemic. In conclusion, digital media contributes to increasing the quality of relationships between Adventist workers and their non-Christian young adult friends.

However, these findings do not explore the impact of digital media on spiritual interaction, which is a key aspect of mission work. Since the context of this research is Christian mission, spiritual interaction is an inevitable element of communication patterns and social dynamics between Adventist workers and MENA youth. In the next chapter, I present key themes of spiritual interactions between Adventist workers and young adults, and I examine digital media's influence on these interactions.

5

Findings: Impact of Digital Media on Spiritual Interaction and Limitations

BECAUSE CHRISTIAN MISSION IS the key context of my research, spirituality related interactions are critical elements of communication patterns and social dynamics among Adventist workers and non-Christian young adults. For example, spiritual conversations are desirable for Adventist workers' non-Christian young adult ministries. In this sense, as with relationship development, spiritual interaction is an important part of communication patterns and social dynamics in relation to my first field research question: "What are Adventist frontline workers' young adult ministry practices for relationship building and spiritual interaction?" In this chapter, I examine key themes of spiritual interaction among Adventist workers and young adults. I also discuss how digital communication media (DCM) relates to this spiritual-interaction process.

SPIRITUAL-INTERACTION PROCESS

The process of spiritual interaction is deeply connected with relationship development. Deep spiritual interaction requires established relationships and trust that enable non-Christian young adults to ask sensitive questions and Adventist workers to answer those questions. Table 5.1 presents three themes relating to the process of spiritual interaction.

Part Two: Field Research

Table 5.1: Spiritual-Interaction Process

Category	Theme	Code	Total Number of Interviewees
Spiritual-interaction process	Start by questions and issues	Religious questions	29
		Life issues	24
	Develop through established trust and curiosity	Trust	20
		Curiosity	12
	Engage in spiritual topics	Prayer	13
		Character of God	12

Start by Questions and Issues

One finding in relation to the first research question is that religious questions and life issues provide the most frequent opportunities for Adventist workers to begin spiritual interactions with young adults. During the semi-structured interview process, twenty-nine out of forty workers mentioned that they were able to start spiritual conversations through asking or receiving religious questions (see table 5.1). Of the survey participants, forty-one Adventist workers responded that religious inquiries from young adults in the Middle East and North Africa (MENA) opened the door for them to introduce spiritual topics (see Q45 in appendix C).

According to Adventist workers, receiving religious questions is not unusual in MENA. One worker mentioned, "In my experience, 90 percent of my non-Christian friends usually ask me about my religion and related topics from the first day" (AW-18). Another worker explained that spiritual or religious topics are not sensitive issues, because those topics are embedded in the daily lives of people in MENA. She observed,

> Something good in this part of the world is like that religion is part of the daily life. Interestingly, in my home country, I have to be more careful to talk about religion, but in here, they are willing to talk about religious matters. I meet people in this country, and they ask me in the first conversation: "Are you a Christian or

Findings: Impact of Digital Media on Spiritual Interaction and Limitations

are you a Muslim? Are you this or that? What do you believe?" (AW-29)

One Adventist Muslim-background believer (MBB) reflected on this phenomenon: "Our Muslim friends, they have so many occasions where they focus so much on spirituality, like in the month of Ramadan or during the Eid" (MBB-51). MENA young adults have little to no aversion to asking and receiving religious questions.

In another instance, several workers were able to initiate spiritual interactions when MENA young adults brought their life issues to Adventist workers. Of the survey participants, thirty-seven Adventist workers responded that life issues created opportunities for them to interact with young adults about spiritual topics (see Q45 in appendix C). Twenty-four out of forty interviewees mentioned young adults' life issues as providing the most frequent opportunities for spiritual interaction (see table 5.1).

One worker reflected on how he usually could share spiritual messages with his friends:

> When people are suffering with something—like some struggles in their family, some issues with their brothers or sisters, or some issues at work—we try to explain to them that God has a plan for everyone. And we start to connect. We start to introduce God in their lives. (AW-4)

In a similar vein, a worker who used to serve in a North African country shared his story about how he began a Bible study with his neighbor:

> I remember the people downstairs, and the guy was like—they were in a huge fight. They were a married couple, and the guy was choking his wife, and I could hear screaming. The husband came up and wanted me to play the mediator. And we were able to have a Bible study with the husband, on like love and true love. So when there was a crisis—when there was a health crisis, a marriage crisis, a relationship crisis, a financial crisis—that's when people are the most open to talk about spiritual topics. (AW-2)

Another worker described an experience with a classmate who went through difficult times: "We were talking together in class. I was able to share about Daniel in the Bible and how God saved him from lions" (AW-34). Reinforcing this finding, during the focus group discussion, an Adventist MBB remarked, "I think life issues could ignite the spiritual conversation" (MBB-51).

Part Two: Field Research

A notable observation is that religious questions and life issues provide different types of spiritual interaction and depth. As I described earlier, religious questions usually lead to introductory conversations about religious identity and ritual. Compared to other parts of the world, in MENA those questions do not require deep trust or relationship. However, the sharing of sensitive life issues does require trust, and once this trust is established, it can lead to in-depth interactions about the Christian message, as illustrated above. Another implication is that openly sharing life issues is an indication of young adults' deep trust in Adventist workers. Figure 5.1 shows the relationship between the key themes in relationship building and in the spiritual-interaction process.

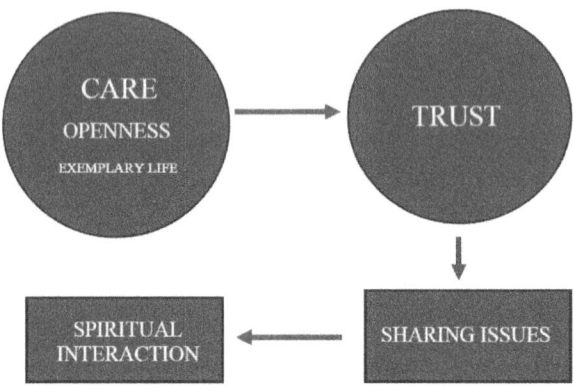

Figure 5.1: Key Factors for Initiating Spiritual Interaction

Develop Through Established Trust and Curiosity

Many workers mentioned that their spiritual interactions with young adults deepened and were propelled forward by previously established trust and curiosity (see table 5.1). Of the survey participants, forty-five responded that previously built trust catalyzed and grew their spiritual interactions with young adults (see Q46 in appendix C). Also, twenty-nine survey participants chose curiosity as the most critical factor to deepen spiritual interaction between Adventist workers and young adults (see Q46 in appendix C).

One participant explained that when Adventist workers established trustworthy relationships, it impacted MENA young adults' receptivity to

Findings: Impact of Digital Media on Spiritual Interaction and Limitations

spiritual messages. He commented, "If they really feel comfortable with us, our spiritual messages are more likely to touch their hearts" (AW-15). A female worker remarked, "They trusted me with some of their spiritual questions, and they had seen something in me that they were willing to ask specific questions" (AW-10).

An established trust enables Adventist workers to bring deeper spiritual topics to MENA young adults. One female worker noted, "If I already have some trust built, we get to the point. They understand that I have some spiritual interests, and they are comfortable" (AW-41). That can even accelerate the initiation of spiritual interaction. One worker explained that after a few casual interactions in which he demonstrated that he was a trustworthy person, he was able to start a Bible study with a young adult. He remarked, "The process was so quick because we had already built trust" (AW-6).

Curiosity is also an important factor to deepen spiritual interactions between Adventist workers and young adults (see table 5.1). One worker reflected on this curiosity and how it moved the process: "Normally the topics will never finish. One question will bring another question" (AW-45). Several workers said that when the young adults to whom they minister start asking more questions, they recognize that as a time to go deeper. One worker remarked, "After some interactions, I don't ask for another appointment or meeting. I wait for them to ask, 'Can you do that again? Can you do that again?'" (AW-25). One MBB's experience reinforces these observations. She noted, "I was so curious, and I had a lot of questions. I asked my Adventist friends a lot of questions, and I kept seeking answers" (MBB-48).

Engage in Spiritual Topics

According to Adventist workers who participated in the semi-structured interviews, prayer and the character of God are two of the most stimulating out of fourteen topics, which also include the purpose of life, sabbath, salvation, human suffering, Jesus, the authenticity of the Bible, world religion, end-time events, creation, dreams and visions, prophets, and religious ritual (see table 5.1). Table 5.2 presents the five most used spiritual topics for engaging with young adults that the survey participants chose.

Part Two: Field Research

Table 5.2: Most Used Spiritual Topics Survey

Top Five Topics	Total Number of Respondents
Prayer	22
Character of God	17
Sabbath	11
Purpose of life	10
Jesus	9

In their survey responses, Adventist worker participants indicated prayer as the spiritual topic most frequently used for engaging with MENA young adults (see table 5.2). Twenty-two out of fifty-one respondents indicated this topic as the one they most frequently initiate. Although MENA young adults recognize the difference between Christian and Muslim prayer, prayer is a ritual practiced by Muslims, so it is often neutral or less sensitive than other spiritual topics. One worker explained,

> I believe that the community here, they already pray for each other. Not in the way that we pray for each other, but yes, at least when we start telling them that we pray for them, they also tell that they are praying for us. So I think it's normal for them. (AW-12)

The establishment of trust-based relationships means that Adventist workers are invited into the life issues and challenges of MENA young adults, which can be an in-road to offer prayers. One worker offered to pray with a young adult friend who was grieving for a deceased family member. She reflected,

> When my friend lost her grandfather, I started sharing with her a lot of biblical messages of how God is able to comfort our hearts— how God is able to give us peace. I told her, "I will pray with you right now." The prayer made a big difference. (AW-16)

One male worker shared similar thoughts: "When they face some problems or some things happening to their life, I usually tell them, 'I would like to pray for you'" (AW-23). One worker shared his story:

> I could pray with people a lot in these crises. Like, my local language teacher was having a problem to have a child and had so

many miscarriages, and the baby died. And then we started praying and she was able to have a baby. So they needed to see God's power in the crises in their lives. (AW-2)

The spiritual topic mentioned next most frequently is God's character (see table 5.2). Seventeen out of fifty-one survey respondents to this question chose this topic as the spiritual subject they use most often when engaging with non-Christian young adults.

In the interviews, several Adventist workers mentioned young adults who struggle with the issue of God's character. One worker remarked, "Some of them become atheists or things like that. They are struggling with their faith, so they start to see a different kind of character of God when we start talking about God who cares about us" (AW-14).

Adventist workers noted that the young adults they serve do not initially perceive God's close presence and relationship with humans. One worker shared,

> We start to show them the character of God in a way that they don't know, because for them it's like, okay, God is God—he's there, up. He doesn't have to be anything with us. So we try to share with them like he is not a God that we cannot have a connection with him. We can ask him for things that we want in our lives to develop and to grow. (AW-4)

One MBB shared the perception of God she had when she was a Muslim:

> I was a strict Muslim. I really kept praying, fasting, and reading the Qur'an. However, I was really stressed, and I could not find rest in my heart, peace in my heart. Then later, when I read the Bible, I really felt the relationship between me and God. It's really different. When I was a Muslim, I was like, "Oh, okay, I'm doing this and that because I don't want God to punish me." Now I know God loves me as I love my child. (MBB-46)

According to Adventist workers who participated in the interviews, young adults' personal issues (for example, challenges with jobs or relationships) often create an opening to introduce the subject of God's character. According to one female worker, "They say, for example, 'I don't like my career, but this is the only thing I can afford. Why doesn't God show me the better way?'" (AW-29).

The above illustrations show that God's character is a critical topic for MENA young adults who live in the uncertain period of the post-Arab

Part Two: Field Research

Spring. Another noteworthy observation is that MENA young adults often believe that their personal well-being in jobs and relationships reflects God's character. Because of this, when they experience unsatisfactory circumstances, they are more likely to engage in spiritual reflections on God's will. This enables Adventist workers to initiate deeper spiritual conversations with their young adult friends.

IMPACT OF DCM ON SPIRITUAL INTERACTION

I discovered key themes in relation to the impact of DCM on spiritual interaction among Adventist workers and young adults as the second part of the second field question: "How is DCM impacting Adventist workers' young adult ministry practices?" To this end, I explored Adventist workers' experiences of using DCM in spiritual interaction with young adults (see table 5.3).

Table 5.3: Impact of DCM on Spiritual Interaction

Category	Theme	Code	Total Number of Interviewees
Impact of DCM on spiritual interactions	Promote spiritual interaction	Enables spiritual interaction online	35
		Provides security	26

Adventist workers utilize DCM for spiritual interactions with young adults. The workers mentioned two major roles of DCM for spiritual interactions with non-Christian friends: (1) it enables spiritual interaction online and (2) provides security. In the following subsections, I describe how each role contributes to promoting spiritual interaction between Adventist workers and young adults.

Enables Spiritual Interaction Online

Many workers mentioned that DCM enabled spiritual interaction with MENA young adults. Thirty-five out of forty interviewees said that DCM allowed them to interact with non-Christians about spiritual topics (see table 5.3). Of the survey participants, twenty-five Adventist workers responded that during the twelve months prior to September 28, 2020, they communicated with young adult friends about spiritual subjects once a week or more

Findings: Impact of Digital Media on Spiritual Interaction and Limitations

via DCM (see Q27 in appendix C). The frequency of these spiritual interactions on DCM is possibly the result of increased digital interactions due to COVID-19 restrictions. Forty-eight of the fifty-one survey participants responded that their digital communication with young adults increased during the COVID-19 pandemic (see Q54 in appendix C).

DCM allows Adventist workers to stimulate young adults' interest and prepares them for deeper interaction. Interviewees described various ways they interact on DCM with non-Christians about spiritual topics. One worker explained that digital media helps the young adults he works with to become familiar with spiritual content:

> DCM gives me the opportunity to share things on my social media that are not necessarily targeted to [young adult friends], but they are exposed to that. But as soon as they see those kinds of information, it can trigger interest, and they send me a message later. (AW-14)

Another worker explained how his social media account allowed him to relate to young adult friends spiritually. He remarked, "I share something on my Facebook, and someone would come and comment, like, 'I agree with this' or 'I don't agree with this'" (AW-40).

Workers utilize DCM not only for sharing light spiritual content but also for deeper spiritual interactions, such as Bible studies. One female Adventist worker reflected,

> [Through DCM,] I interacted with my friend who was showing signs of being very depressed and wanting to commit suicide. . . . Likewise, I do Bible studies through WhatsApp conversation instead of sitting down and opening a Bible. That is how I'm sharing the word of God. (AW-16)

Another worker actively utilizes text messages for Bible study with his young adult friends. He described,

> We do Bible studies on Messenger. Sometimes I send Bible verses by WhatsApp and ask them to read. To make sure that they read it, I ask them to send me the reflection on what they read and what they understood from the verses. (AW-15)

One worker shared a story of how she employed DCM in order to minster to fifteen female friends in her ministry circle. She explained,

Part Two: Field Research

> We were having almost daily communication with a group of about fifteen women. We would send encouraging messages to each other. They would talk with each other. They would send little videos that they found or Bible verses. And then we started, as a group, preparing our own Bible verses on nature pictures and then making a two- to three-minute video, probably a one- to two-minute video, actually explaining the verse or how we understood it or what lessons we could learn from it. (AW-5)

DCM enables Adventist workers to stimulate young adults' interests in spiritual topics, and it provides Adventist workers with interactive ways of carrying out spiritual nurturing. Several Adventist MBBs supported the Adventist workers' experiences. According to one MBB, "The biggest value is that you can get more [spiritual] knowledge. When you have a question, you can quickly send it to one of the leaders or someone who knows the Bible better so that he can explain to you. Yeah, this is the important thing" (MBB-49).

Provides Security

Adventist workers also observed that DCM provides them with safe platforms that allow them to avoid direct conflicts and security issues when they share spiritual messages with young adults. Twenty-six out of forty interviewees mentioned that DCM provided Adventist workers and young adults security for spiritual conversations (see table 5.3).

Several Adventist workers said that by using DCM, they were able to avoid conflict when they were sharing messages of which they were uncertain about the reception. One worker explained how through DCM he is able to protect the relationships with his young friends when he must answer difficult questions about Christianity. He reflected,

> We would have liked some kind of difficult questions that can be answered, for example: "Is Jesus God?" Or talking about their own religion. I could share videos that can answer such questions on WhatsApp. I would not be comfortable to answer that question directly as a friend because maybe it can create problems between us. Maybe it's a very hard topic that can destroy our relationship if I would talk with them in person. But I can share a video with them on DCM. (AW-6)

Findings: Impact of Digital Media on Spiritual Interaction and Limitations

Because of the way communication on DCM occurs, MENA young adults have the freedom to engage or disengage with sensitive topics. One worker noted, "The person has a choice of accepting the message or not" (AW-40).

According to interviewees, Adventist workers are able to maintain confidentiality through digital communication with young adult friends; this, in turn, allows them to share deep spiritual topics without security concerns. One worker shared his story:

> We cannot discuss private things at school. And you can't deepen a relationship or a friendship if you only discuss homework and you only talk during breaks in the school. So this privacy, which Messenger offers, especially for discussing religious questions, makes people much more open in this culture. (AW-33)

Another worker described the following:

> I would say that [DCM] ... makes people feel safer about learning this new information about praying, and I think it is safer for them because it's more like I'm here, but I'm not here. It helped a lot for us to break through cultural barriers that you wouldn't easily break in person, that the social pressure wouldn't let you in, but technology can make you invisible. (AW-43)

Adventist MBBs who participated in the focus group discussion supported the accounts of the Adventist workers. One MBB stated,

> I can guarantee that they will have the freedom of questioning and doubting [on DCM]. And that's what's most important, because usually when we are confronted by the society, we are afraid to change because we are going to be judged by our family. We can be threatened. We can be, I mean, [critiqued by] the society. But social media, what it gives, it gives confidence and freedom to doubt. And this doubting will push them to ask more questions. (MBB-50)

DCM enables Adventist workers to interact with young adults about spiritual topics and to share sensitive messages while avoiding direct conflicts. It also allows young adults to share deep spiritual questions with their Adventist friends without security concerns. Of the survey respondents, thirty-eight answered that DCM has been moderately, very, or extremely effective for spiritual interaction with their young adult friends (see Q47 in appendix C).

Part Two: Field Research

LIMITATIONS OF DCM FOR YOUNG ADULT MINISTRY PRACTICES

Investigating only the positive impacts of DCM does not provide a whole picture. Therefore, I scrutinized the limitations of DCM for Adventist workers' young adult ministry practices. In the same vein, I also attempted to answer the third field question: "What are the non-replaceable roles of in-person communication (IPC) in Adventist workers' young adult ministry practices?" Table 5.4 presents the two themes in the category of the negative impact of DCM on young adult ministry: exhaustion and lack of depth, and lack of human touch.

Table 5.4: Limitations of DCM

Category	Theme	Code	Total Number of Interviewees
Limitations of DCM for young adult ministry practices	Exhaustion and lack of depth	Time consuming	16
		Shallow conversation and relationship	11
	Lack of human touch	Physical behaviors	33
		Focused interaction	6

Exhaustion and Lack of Depth

While DCM positively relates to Adventist workers' young adult ministry practices, it can also produce adverse effects. Seventeen out of forty interviewees mentioned that using DCM can be excessively time-consuming (see table 5.4). Twenty-seven out of the fifty-one survey participants responded that DCM negatively affected their lives because of how much time it took out of their days (see Q40 in appendix C).

Many workers pointed out that they tend to spend time using DCM excessively and unconsciously. One worker commented, "You are so into the network and the internet, browsing and browsing and browsing. Finally, you find that you are lost somewhere. You don't even realize how much time you spent" (AW-32). Similar to this, one worker shared his experience about how DCM overuse brought about burnout:

Findings: Impact of Digital Media on Spiritual Interaction and Limitations

> WhatsApp is the main one. I know they like to talk to me. Friendship here is very demanding in time and attention. I am still struggling to balance because you're burning out. You also have other things to do and you just don't want to be talking [on DCM]. (AW-27)

One frontline worker described how she set aside time to fast from her digital device in order to limit the time she spent on DCM:

> It feels like you always have to be attached to your phone. I've set up some boundaries for that. There are times that I even do a whole day of no cell phone. There are times that I feel like, okay, enough—it's too much. And I have to do that once a week sometimes. (AW-10)

Several workers mentioned a distraction issue, which is caused by the constant use of DCM. One female worker shared her experience and evaluation of DCM in connection with ministry:

> [DCM] is a big distraction in many ways. There's so much to take your time and to take your energy, you know, Facebook and all these things. Many times, we're so busy checking our phones we miss out on other opportunities that we could have connected with people. (AW-5)

Too much time spent using DCM adversely affects Adventist workers' spiritual lives. One Adventist worker described his addiction to DCM and how it interrupted his spiritual time with God. He explained,

> I feel that it has become a habit for me to check in my WhatsApp almost automatically. It's a sort of addiction almost. Like I am curious about what's new and who contacted me. And it disturbs my quiet times, sometime in the morning, the habit of looking—I have this real struggle of watching myself when I don't want to check my cell phone until I have my time with the Lord, but it's become almost like a natural reflex. So this is a negative aspect of it. (AW-20)

As I mentioned earlier, Adventist workers' DCM use increased during the COVID-19 pandemic. This implies that Adventist workers could experience more negative aspects of DCM use during the pandemic. One female worker described how she dealt with the problem of DCM becoming too time-consuming during the COVID-19 lockdown:

Part Two: Field Research

> When COVID started, I deleted the YouTube app from my phone. And I couldn't believe how much of a difference that made in my day-to-day life. Before that, if I had a spare minute or a spare second, I found myself checking like, what are the new little videos or news clips or whatever. I do not plan on putting it back on my phone just from a personal perspective. (AW-8)

Another negative element of DCM is that in their young adult ministries, some workers experienced their relationships and conversations with young adults on DCM as shallow. Eleven interviewees mentioned the lack of depth in communication (see table 5.4). Similarly, in the survey, fifteen participants responded that DCM contributed to shallow conversations and relationships for young adult ministry (see Q40 in appendix C).

One worker noted, "You are just friends on Instagram or Facebook. But there's no personal contact that I would really wish to have. It's just that we're friends on Facebook and Instagram" (AW-34). Another worker questioned the quality of digital communication:

> Young adults communicate without real communication on DCM. That's a challenge. You are part of a WhatsApp group. They see our messages, and then occasionally, they'll send a brief yes or no, or okay. You may feel that communication has happened, but really it hasn't. Just because you're informed doesn't mean that we've communicated. It is very normal to have these kinds of interactions [on DCM]. (AW-9)

One worker observed that DCM does not encourage Adventist workers to develop deeper interaction. He remarked, "So the negative could be perhaps the temptation of feeling that [DCM] is enough. I have done my part since I've shared things through WhatsApp. However, this should be just a step in the process" (AW-21).

Lack of Human Touch

If I investigate only what DCM can do for young adult ministry, it does not provide a complete picture of Adventist workers' communication patterns. Therefore, I examined the limitations of digital communication that only IPC can provide. Many workers commented that human touch is one of the key factors that DCM cannot contribute to Adventist workers' young adult ministries.

Findings: Impact of Digital Media on Spiritual Interaction and Limitations

PHYSICAL BEHAVIORS

Although DCM has an important role in Adventist workers' young adult ministry practices, many workers stated that physical behaviors—touch, use of space, facial expressions, and gestures—cannot be replaced by digital communication. Thirty-three out of forty interviewees mentioned that physical behaviors are critical elements of IPC that cannot fully be conveyed by DCM (see table 5.4). Forty-two out of fifty-one survey participants responded that physical behaviors are the most critical roles of IPC in their young adult ministries (see Q49 in appendix C).

One worker explained about the importance of nonverbal communication that can only occur in person. He remarked, "There's a limit when you cannot hug, when you cannot see the tears running down their cheeks, or they cannot see my emotional reaction to that" (AW-44). Another worker commented that the significance of IPC is not only about visuality but also about sensibility by co-location. She remarked, "It's not that you can't see them. You can, if you have a video call. You can see them. But, yeah, there are some limitations, like touch[ing], putting a hand on their shoulder, and hugging" (AW-45). These illustrations indicate that IPC and digital communication play supplementary roles in Adventist workers' young adult ministries. Adventist MBBs in the focus group discussion supported Adventist workers' experiences of IPC. One MBB stated,

> I totally agree with [the Adventist workers]. I would say that showing emotions to others in person is important. One person started crying, and we just needed to give him a hug [during our small group]. You cannot do that on screen, just to give a hug to the person and that he feels embraced. (MBB-51)

FOCUSED INTERACTION

According to Adventist workers, IPC allows for focused interaction when they communicate with young adults. Although only six interviewees mentioned this during the semi-structured interviews (see table 5.4), twenty-four out of fifty-one survey participants answered that one of the important roles of IPC is that it eliminates distractions and allows them to focus on interactions with young adults (see Q49 in appendix C).

One worker described the benefit of IPC: "When I'm in in-person meetings, I dedicate 100 percent of my time to them. I don't pay attention to social media—to any distractions or to the phone or anything else. I'm just with them, and I give my full attention" (AW-14). Another worker

Part Two: Field Research

shared similar thoughts about her Bible study with young adult friends: "If you're face-to-face and you sit down, you can go through the Bible together without the distractions" (AW-5).

SUMMARY

In this chapter, I presented key themes of Adventist workers' spiritual-interaction process, which is the second part of their communication patterns and social dynamics. Adventist workers initiated spiritual interaction with young adults most frequently through religious questions and life issues. In MENA, introductory conversations based on religious questions about religious identity and ritual do not require deep trust or relationship; however, when MENA young adults share their life issues with Adventist workers, this can build trust that leads to in-depth interactions about biblical messages. Young adults become willing to share their innermost life issues when trust is built through Adventist workers' care, openness, and exemplary lives.

Another finding is that spiritual interactions among Adventist workers and young adults are deepened and moved forward through establishing trust-based relationships and engaging the natural curiosity of MENA young adults. The most engaging spiritual topics are prayer and God's character, because those two subjects are what young adults desire answers to when they deal with unsolved life questions.

Based on this, I presented key themes of DCM's impact on Adventist workers' spiritual interaction with MENA young adults, which is the second part of their communication patterns and social dynamics. DCM enables Adventist workers to hold spiritual conversations with young adult friends, and it also allows them to avoid direct conflicts when they share sensitive messages with friends. Through DCM, young adults are able to interact with Adventist workers for deep spiritual questions without security concerns. The above illustrations also imply that DCM can alleviate social and cultural pressure for young adults.

Although DCM positively contributes to Adventist workers' deepening relationships of trust and dialogue, it also can negatively affect their ministries. While DCM allows Adventist workers to connect with their young adult friends regardless of the time and space, it frequently leads to distraction and addiction, becoming time-consuming. In addition, on DCM, some Adventist workers experience shallow conversations and relationships with young adults. In order to equip Adventist workers with

Findings: Impact of Digital Media on Spiritual Interaction and Limitations

digital media model practices, the church needs to be aware of both the positives and negatives of DCM.

DCM is not a panacea for all the challenges of young adult ministry. IPC is also a significant part of young adult ministry practices and plays a vital role in communication between Adventist workers and young adults. While DCM can strengthen the relationship between Adventist workers and young adults, IPC allows for emotional bonding through physical behaviors that cannot be replaced by digital communication. IPC also allows Adventist workers to focus on interactions with young adults without distractions. IPC and DCM are supplementary in Adventist workers' relationship building with non-Christian young adults.

Although I discovered findings about the impact of digital media on relationship building and spiritual interactions, chapters 4 and 5 do not discuss how those findings advanced the theoretical constructs in the literature review. Thus, in the next chapter, I discuss findings in the light of my literature review to demonstrate the relevance of the review, and I exhibit implications of the findings for my application.

6

Reflections on Theoretical Constructs and Applications

IN THE PREVIOUS CHAPTER, I presented key findings from interviews, a focus group, and a survey in relation to my four field research questions. In this chapter, first, I discuss findings in light of the literature review in order to show how the theoretical constructs can be applied to the findings.

Second, I briefly demonstrate implications of key findings for application. This discussion provides a foundation for answering my application intent question: "What digital media practices can be developed to strengthen Adventist frontline workers' relationship building and spiritual interactions with young adult non-Christians?"

DISCUSSION OF THE FINDINGS IN LIGHT OF THE LITERATURE

I based the design of this field research on key theories surrounding the relationships between communication patterns, social dynamics, and deepening relationships among Adventist workers and non-Christian young adults in the Middle East and North Africa (MENA). In this section, I discuss how the findings relate to the literature reviewed in chapters 1 and 2.

Socializing Technology

In chapter 1, I demonstrated the impact of sociality-related traits of digital media on human relationships. According to theologian Angela Gorrell, the younger generation has a way of "socializing' technology," and they use digital media to foster relationships with their friends.¹ Although Gorrell's theory of socializing technology asserts the importance of digital media for socializing among youth, it does not provide adequate information about how the media is involved in the process of relationship building. To fill this gap, my findings show how digital media influences relationship-building processes among non-Christian young adults and our frontline workers. One worker observed, "I meet you one day, five minutes ago, and then you just ask me my Facebook or my Instagram. But here [in MENA], it is really the way that they [young adults] communicate" (AW-34). Although first encounters take place in person, the exchange of social media account information is vital to thoroughly enter a relationship. This indicates that digital media can be utilized to deepen relationships. In this sense, the term *socializing technology* encompasses fundamental sociality-related characteristics of digital media that several scholars describe.

The first trait is open communication, or freedom of communication. Robert D. Putnam suggests that a core characteristics of the internet is open communication, in that it allows individuals to be more candid and it levels the playing field, which does not happen in face-to-face meetings.² Manuel Castells points out that individual open communication has become the predominant practice among media users.³ This means that digital media enables people to express their thoughts, opinions, and feelings regardless of established authorities and social pressures. According to Putnam, anonymity is a precondition of open communication on digital media, because people become more honest when digital media does not reveal much information about them.⁴ However, according to Luciano Floridi, not all non-anonymous digital communications are inauthentic, because when people interact on digital media—whether anonymously or openly—they affect their authentic self-identities.⁵ I conclude that digital media offers individuals a platform to express their true selves, both anonymously and openly. In addition, this type of candid communication affects the quality of relationships by allowing individuals to reveal their weaknesses. Patti M. Valkenburg and Jochen Peter argue that online self-disclosure enhances the quality of a relationship

1. Gorrell, *Always On*, 14.
2. Putnam, *Bowling Alone*, 186.
3. Castells, *Internet Galaxy*, 54.
4. Putnam, *Bowling Alone*, 186.
5. Floridi, *Fourth Revolution*.

because the act of sharing something sensitive exhibits deep trust in others and thus creates a sense of connectedness.[6]

Although I stated that full anonymity of digital media is not an essential factor for open communication, my findings demonstrate the importance of anonymity (which means hiding one's real identity) or confidentiality of digital media for young adults in MENA to engage in open communication. One worker described, "My friends don't speak much about their ideas and how they view things in real life. But then when they go on social media, they start expressing their frustrations, even with religion" (AW-16). One Adventist Muslim-background believer (MBB) explained, "We can be threatened. We can be, I mean, [critiqued by society]. But social media, what it gives, it gives confidence and freedom to doubt" (MBB-50). One precondition for those comments is that the users of digital media did not have to disclose their real identities online, or their digital interactions remained confidential. This indicates that digital media's anonymity or confidentiality plays a critical role in allowing Adventist workers and MBBs to speak their genuine thoughts and opinions more openly than they are able to in offline communication, considering social and religious pressures in the region. Out of these examples, one significant point is that such digital anonymity or confidentiality may provide non-Christian young adults with security so they can be open to online spiritual discussions. Also, this security may allow non-Christian young adults to engage in online self-disclosure that will increase the quality of their relationships with Adventist workers as they create bonds and foster a sense of trust.

The second key theory is the connectivity of digital media. Communication scholars Richard Seyler Ling and Jonathan Donner argue that the digital technology of mobile communication offers individuals flexibility, accessibility, and availability because everybody is addressable and connectable through the media.[7] Ling and Donner state that the value of connectivity has impacted social relationships by the assumption that "all of us are available" regardless of time and space.[8] The connectivity theory implies that digital media may create a sense of connectedness among different social groups by overcoming the barriers of time and space. However, because the connectivity that Ling and Donner discuss focuses on technological connectability, it is limited to a functional aspect of digital

6. Valkenburg and Peter, "Social Consequences."
7. Ling and Donner, *Mobile Communication*, 3, 135.
8. Ling and Donner, *Mobile Communication*, 135.

media. It does not answer the question of how digital media's connectivity affects emotional connectedness or a sense of togetherness.

In answer to the question above, my findings demonstrate how digital media's connectivity fosters a feeling of togetherness and care among Adventist workers and their non-Christian young adult friends by overcoming barriers of time and space, enabling them to check on each other frequently. One frontline worker explained the importance of digital media for nurturing relationships regardless of time and space: "You have an opportunity to enter that person's life that God can use—at any moment of the day" (AW-2). Another worker commented, "The biggest thing of digital communication media is that it gives a feeling that I am always connected with my non-Christian friends" (AW-18). Digital media enables Christian workers to connect with their non-Christian friends. Further, it allows them, with love and care, to support their non-Christian young adult friends in times of crisis. The way in which digital media allows individuals to be constantly together and care for one another can be seen as a reflection of the omnipresent God. The mechanical connectivity of digital media is not central to deepening relationships of trust and dialogue—the real factor is Adventist workers' willingness to care for and support their non-Christian young adult friends by utilizing the connectivity of digital media. Through this, they can foster a sense of togetherness that can develop relationships of trust and dialogue.

The third theory involves the interplay between digital media—social networking sites in particular—with real life. Digital media interactions can be connected to offline life, which can, in turn, impact friendship development.[9] For example, new graduates continue to communicate on social media after graduation, and such practice allows them to maintain their preexisting offline relationships online. However, danah boyd's theory of interplay between digital media and real-life relationships does not touch on how digital media impacts emotional depth of relationships. boyd's example is that alumni continue to maintain and develop their preexisting relationships by sharing job information or chatting online. Although this displays how digital media can affect the maintenance or development of offline relationships, it does not offer adequate information about the relationship between digital media and emotional depth of relationships. I argued in the literature review that the use of digital media can extend beyond the mere maintenance of existing social relationships—it can also

---

9. boyd, "Friendship," 79, 113.

Part Two: Field Research

deepen relationships of trust through the interplay between online and offline communications. For example, although teachers and students have preexisting real-life relationships, when they continue to communicate directly with one another on a daily basis through digital media, this increases a sense of togetherness.[10] These points indicate that continual online and offline hybrid communications can deepen relationships. Sarah Schwartz et al.'s example of teacher-student relationships also implies that a desire for ongoing hybrid communication is an important factor in increasing the quality of relationships.

My findings show that in the MENA context in which I serve, both online and offline communications are needed to impact relationships among Christian workers and their non-Christian friends. For example, the use of digital media without offline relationships does not impact the relationship-building process. In the semi-structured interviews, only three workers mentioned that they could initiate relationships through the use of digital media. This shows that digital media's role in relationship building is not effective without offline interactions. However, the mere use of both online and offline communication may not guarantee the enhancement of a sense of emotional togetherness. My findings suggest that Adventist workers' willingness to and intention of using both forms of communication are important. One worker emphasized how checking in on non-Christian friends via digital media is critical for nurturing relationships, even if he meets with his friends every day in person (AW-1). Another worker commented, "We cannot maintain relationships if we don't send messages. When I send them a message, we keep our relationship" (AW-20). These comments show not only the importance of using both online and offline communications for Adventist workers' relationship building with non-Christian young adults, but they also hint at the workers' intention to use both. When workers want to express care for their friends through this hybrid form of communication, the practice increases a sense of care and togetherness, which deepens relationships of trust and dialogue. This enhanced trust enables Adventist workers to share God's redemptive love with non-Christian young adults while mitigating the risk of misunderstanding. Therefore, the interplay between offline and online communications advances kingdom building.

The above discussions indicate that the findings about how digital media affects relationship-building processes among Adventist workers

10. Schwartz et al., "Mentoring in the Digital Age."

and non-Christian young adults are relevant to the literature reviewed in chapter 1. In addition, these discussions fill the gaps that exist in the literature. My findings indicate that digital media allows Adventist workers and non-Christian young adults to deepen relationships of trust and dialogue through open communication and the fostering of a sense of connectedness and trust. However, my findings not only deal with the bright side of digital media, but they also address its downsides.

Downsides of Digital Media

In chapter 1, as I discussed the sociality-related traits of digital media, I demonstrated the negative aspects of digital media, such as overuse of digital technology, distraction, and shallow relationships.[11] While scholars argue about digital media's negative impacts on personal lives and relationships, my field research specifically explored how digital media interferes with Adventist workers' ministry practices for non-Christian young adults. One worker described how digital media captures the workers' attention for a long time: "You are so into the network and the internet—browsing and browsing and browsing. Finally, you find that you are lost somewhere. You don't even realize how much time you spent" (AW-32). Another worker observed the shallowness of this form of communication: "You are just friends on Instagram or Facebook. But there's no personal contact that I would really wish to have. It's just that we're friends on Facebook and Instagram" (AW-34). One MBB indicated that the lack of in-person communication and human touch was a downside of digital media: "One person started crying, and we just needed to give him a hug [during our small group]. You cannot do that on [a] screen—just to give a hug to the person and that he feels embraced" (MBB-51). These comments display two key issues of digital media for gospel workers: (1) it is time consuming, or addictive, and (2) it lacks in-person interaction. If I consider the nature and purpose of missionary work in the region, these two issues cannot be overlooked. For example, building trustworthy relationships is essential to delivering persuasive gospel messages to non-Christians in MENA, because direct or public evangelism is avoided. In this sense, the lack of in-person interaction and human touch can hinder the communication of spiritual messages due to the ways in which it limits depth of relationship and the building of trust.

---

11. Auxier et al., "Parenting Children"; Rushkoff, *Program or Be Programmed*; Turkle, *Alone Together*.

Part Two: Field Research

I propose that in order to avoid such issues, Adventist workers need to be aware of both positives and negatives of digital media, and they need continually to observe and reflect on digital media rather than indiscriminately embrace the technology. To address the negative impacts of digital media on depth of relationship, I intend to identify certain digital media practices that may help our frontline workers recognize and avoid those issues.

The findings I described above regarding the shortcomings of digital media are relevant to the literature I reviewed in chapter 1. Through the field research, I further explored how digital media limits one of the Adventist workers' core tasks for sharing the gospel of Jesus Christ in MENA: building trustworthy relationships with non-Christian young adults. I intend to identify digital media practices to mitigate these issues for Adventist workers.

Attitudes and Values of the Younger Generation

In chapter 2, I described the attitudes and values that characterize social dynamics of the younger generation in the post-Arab Spring period. In the light of the Arab Spring and the post-Arab Spring context, uncertainty and anxiety are two major outcomes of political and economic instabilities. Uncertainty and anxiety resulted in two central attitudes of MENA young people: (1) desire for personal success, and (2) desire for trustworthy relationships.[12] In chapter 1, I demonstrated that young people in the MENA context are more concerned about their personal well-being than they are about a group agenda, and they also are seeking trustworthy relationships.[13]

Beverley Milton-Edwards explains how even traditional youth in Jordan desire the collapse of the current impractical and unstable social system, because they cannot rely on the political, economic, and public systems of the country.[14] This shows why the youth have become more individualistic than before. Young people rely on individual efforts for achieving success instead of depending on institutions and systems. This suggests that the desire for personal success requires autonomy and freedom of expression because young people want to determine the direction of their own lives, build their own relationship networks, and express

---

12. Gertel and Kreuer, "Values," loc. 1624.
13. Gertel and Kreuer, "Values"; Ouaissa, "Religion."
14. Milton-Edwards, *Marginalized Youth*, 5, 9.

Reflections on Theoretical Constructs and Applications

their own opinions regardless of others' views. In a similar vein, Arab youth perceive religion as a personal issue.[15]

Regarding trust in relationships, Arab youth desire trustworthy friends who both recognize and tolerate them.[16] These relationships can provide youth with emotional and psychological security that traditional political and social systems cannot provide in the post-Arab Spring period. In the literature review, I argued that trustworthy relationships require demonstrations of appreciation, care, and discretion. These points suggest that MENA youth are open to building relationships with people outside their traditional boundaries based on their personal interests and their perception of others' trustworthiness. However, the literature was not able to provide information about specific factors that can stimulate shared interests and build trustworthiness to help in the relationship-building processes between Adventist workers and non-Christian young adults.

To address this gap, my field-research findings indicate that MENA young adults are open to relationships with non-Muslim outsiders if the relationships contribute to their personal growth: for example, if a relationship contributes to the development or learning of various skills. One worker shared that a young non-Christian friend walked into the church for the first time because he overheard the worker playing the guitar and wanted to connect with him—their relationship began through a common love of music (AW-31). Another worker remarked that he has connected with several MENA young adults through shared athletic pursuits (AW-44). These comments show that new skills or helpful activities allow non-Christian young adults to connect and interact with Adventist workers.

My findings also demonstrate that regularly checking in on one's friends online exhibits support, care, and discretion and can boost the quality of relationships. One worker explains how demonstrating his care and support in this way helps him develop relationships with non-Christian young adults in MENA: "They appreciate that a lot, because you remember them, so you send them a message, just saying, 'Hi!' or 'How are you?' They appreciate that" (AW-27). Another worker explained, "And just to know that somebody cares about them, somebody's concerned about their well-being . . . that means a lot to families" (AW-5).

The findings of my field research specify the factors that allow non-Christian young adults to mingle with outsiders and build trustworthy

---

15. Ouaissa, "Religion," loc. 1937.
16. Gertel and Kreuer, "Values," loc. 1444.

relationships with Christians. This indicate that the attitudes and values present in social dynamics impact the deepening of relationships of trust and dialogue. Together with attitudes and values, trust is a critical element of relationship development. I thus explore the relationship between my findings and the literature that outlines general trust-building factors.

Trust-Building Factors

In chapter 2, I examined attributional, cognitive, and risk-taking trust-building factors as part of the social dynamics that may impact the deepening of relationships. I argued that these factors contribute to Adventist workers building deeper trust and relationships with their non-Christian friends, because trust is crucial to beginning and developing any relationship.[17] Scholars suggest three key attributional factors of trustees that can build trust: integrity, benevolence, and competence.[18] In the literature review, I argued that the definition of integrity is the trustees' authenticity or openness about themselves and others. When trustees are open about themselves, the act increases trusters' level of trust toward the trustees. Integrity can also be measured by how faithfully trustees maintain trusters' confidentiality.

Through my evaluation of specific examples in my field research, I determined ways in which trustees' integrity or openness can deepen trust and enhance relationships. A key element of integrity is being vulnerable toward trusters. One worker explained how she gained trust by being open about herself: "When you are real, when you show the real you with your weaknesses and good things, the person trusts you because they feel that you don't hide like others" (AW-37). When Adventist workers become vulnerable to and are transparent with their non-Christian friends, the workers can be perceived as honest friends who do not hide their real selves from others.

Another important element of integrity involves the discretion of the trustee. One interview participant described how being a safe person from whom to seek counsel is another critical element for building trust. Another worker shared a story about how his young adult friends tested his trustworthiness: "When they feel that you are a safe person, it builds up, and then the relationship will be stronger" (AW-15). When Adventist

17. Mishra, "Oganizational Responses to Crisis."
18. Dirks, "Three Fundamental Questions"; Whitener et al., "Managers as Initiators of Trust."

workers guard the confidentiality of their non-Christian friends' inner issues, they become perceived as reliable people. The comments made by the interview participants identify vulnerability and discretion as key elements of behaving with integrity, which can build trust between Adventist workers and non-Christian young adults.

Benevolence is also a critical factor for building trust. Benevolence is reflected through demonstrations of concern about the wellbeing of friends or through a willingness to care for other parties.[19] People begin to trust when the truster observes support and care from the trustee. However, the concept of *care* is broad, and the literature does not provide tangible practices that can display benevolence. I sought to answer that question through my field research. My findings display forms of care that can be critical to building trust and relationships among Adventist workers and their non-Christian young adult friends. One worker explained how, through helping, he earns the trust of his university classmates: "In my class, if someone needs my help, I'm always there. So if someone asks me something, even if it's late or even if I am tired, I always try to do something. I say, 'Okay, let me help you. What do you need?'" (AW-28). When Adventist workers are willing to step in when their friends need help, such behavior demonstrates care and support, which increases the quality of trust.

In the literature review, several scholars stated that cognitive factors allow trusters to build initial trust with trustees through secondhand information from credible friends. Initial trust can also take place when trusters and trustees who otherwise have inadequate experience with one another share common interests and pursue common goals.[20] This has significant implications for Adventist workers in the Middle East and North Africa.

When Adventist workers come to the mission field, there are two obstacles they face as they begin to establish relationships with local non-Christians: (1) they are foreigners, and (2) they are Christians. My findings revealed how Adventist workers' connections help them, as foreigners and Christians, continue to build trust with non-Christian young adults. One worker observed this in the following interactions: "A friend of mine introduced me to his friend, and then the new friend connected me to another friend. In this way, my relationship circle with young adults is getting bigger every year" (AW-38). This finding indicates that one critical way for

---

19. Whitener et al., "Managers as Initiators of Trust," 523.

20. Komiak and Benbasat, "Effects of Personalization"; McKnight and Chervany, "Reflections"; Moysidou and Hausberg, "In Crowdfunding We Trust."

Adventist workers to develop relationships with young adults is through introductions from preexisting common friends.

Further, my findings suggest that sharing common tasks, interests, and goals is also important for Adventist workers, as foreigners and Christians, to build relationships with non-Christian young adults in the region. Connections through language schools, universities, and social clubs offer Adventist workers opportunities to develop initial trust and relationship. One male worker described how sports provided him with the most constant and frequent opportunities to engage with young adult friends. He observed, "There is a group for running, and I met approximately 50 percent of my non-Christian young adult friends through running" (AW-44). This suggests that common interests and goals enable Adventist workers and non-Christian young adults to relate each other in ways that positively affect their relationship development.

In addition to the factors I have discussed that contribute to trust and relationship building, scholars argue that risk, or risk-taking, is not only a result of established trust but also is a factor in building trust in relationships.[21] This indicates that risk and trust are interlinked in the building and deepening of relationships. Although the literature does not answer the question asking how risk-taking impacts Adventist workers' missional activities, my findings display the relationship between risk-taking, trust, and spiritual interaction. The Adventist workers I interviewed observed that when they build trust with their non-Christian young adult friends, it enables them to engage in spiritual interactions that can be sensitive in the region. One worker commented, "If I already have some trust built, we get to the point. They understand that I have some spiritual interests, and they are comfortable" (AW-41). Another worker explained that because he was able to demonstrate that he was a trustworthy person, he was able to start a Bible study with a young adult friend. He observed, "The process was so quick because we had already built trust" (AW-6). This shows recursive dynamics between risk-taking, spiritual interactions, and trust building: risk-taking deepens trust, and built trust enables risk-taking actions.

Our workers and their young adult friends are in an environment that requires them to assume risk when they engage in spiritual conversations. My findings demonstrated how digital media can be involved in these risky spiritual interactions. One worker described how digital media allowed

---

21. Bhattacharya et al., "Formal Model of Trust; Luhmann, "Familiarity, Confidence, Trust"; Rousseau et al., "Not So Different After All."

Reflections on Theoretical Constructs and Applications

him to handle delicate spiritual topics in discussions with non-Christians: "So this privacy, which Messenger offers, especially for discussing religious questions, makes people much more open in this culture" (AW-33). While this indicates the cultural or religious restrictions that the workers and their non-Christian friends face, it also indicates that the restrictive environment offers Adventist workers and their non-Christian friends opportunities to build trust more quickly as they take risks of sharing spiritual conversations. Next, I discuss my findings in the light of application.

IMPLICATIONS OF FINDINGS FOR APPLICATION

My application intent question is "What digital media practices can be identified to strengthen Adventist frontline workers' relationship building and spiritual interactions with young adult non-Christians?" To address this, in this section, I discuss implications of my findings in order to provide primary ideas for application.

My findings show that digital media catalyzes interactions among non-Christian young adults and Adventist workers by providing relevant talking points and allowing them to learn about each other in a short period of time. Adventist workers notice their non-Christian friends' emotional status, life events, and interests through digital media. For example, their non-Christian friends express sadness or happiness on social media. The workers also know information about birthdays, sicknesses, and major life events, such as when their friends attend funerals. Therefore, digital media offers workers opportunities to sympathize, celebrate, and discuss with non-Christian young adult friends. One worker explained how digital media provided her with relevant talking points to create conversations with a non-Christian friend: "Once, someone posted a picture of a crying woman on WhatsApp. I was able to have conversations about the status. I used it to start a new conversation" (AW-45). Comments such as this suggest that digital media model practices should include Adventist workers strategically utilizing digital media to expedite the process of deepening relationships of trust and dialogue with non-Christian young adults. To this end, I hope to identify practical tips and suggestions to maximize the strengths of digital media as Adventist workers enter and develop relationships with non-Christian friends.

The findings also exhibit that digital media allows individuals to experiences care and a sense of togetherness as they and their friends constantly check in on each other, openly participate in self-disclosure, and engage in the sharing of common interests or similar lifestyles. These factors increase the quality of relationships between Adventist workers and their non-Christian young adult friends by enhancing trust. For example, digital self-disclosure or vulnerability is connected to integrity, which is a critical trust-building factor. This means digital communications contribute to deepening relationships of trust and dialogue. Therefore, I endeavored to identify digital media model practices that demonstrate feasible methods to maximize experiences of care and togetherness. We anticipate that when Adventist workers practice these principles, Arab youth will increasingly trust in our workers or gospel messengers, and consequently, this will increase non-Christian young adults' receptivity to the gospel message.

My findings demonstrate that digital media enables spiritual interaction online and provides security for that interaction. When Adventist workers are perceived as trustworthy friends, it allows non-Christian young adults to ask them difficult or sensitive questions without cultural and social pressures—it also enables Adventist workers to answer those questions without harming their relationships. Considering these findings, digital media model practices may indicate appropriate approaches and tactics that can enhance Adventist workers' spiritual interactions with non-Christian young adults as they use the media. Based on the deepened relationships of trust and dialogue, those digital media principles can empower Adventist workers to share God's redemptive plan for humankind with their non-Christian young adult friends.

The findings also display negative aspects of digital media for Adventist workers, such as overuse of the media, lack of depth, and lack of human touch. This means that as our Adventist workers use digital media in the mission field, they must be aware of the shortcomings of the media and constantly reflect on the media's destructive tendencies. I intend to identify digital media model practices that demonstrate methods to mitigate the limitations of the media. Those principles will enable Adventist workers to reflect upon and moderate their use of digital media in the mission field.

SUMMARY

My findings about how digital media as a socializing technology affects relationship-building processes among Adventist workers and non-Christian young adults answer the questions from the literature I reviewed in chapter 1. For example, the findings revealed that using both online and offline communications is more effective than using only digital media to

Reflections on Theoretical Constructs and Applications

catalyze the relationship development. While the literature asserts digital media's contribution to building and nurturing relationships among individuals, my findings display how specific digital media practices impact enhancing trust between Adventist workers and their non-Christian friends. One key point I discovered through the field research is that the workers' willingness to connect, care for, and support their non-Christian friends is more vital for creating a sense of emotional togetherness than is digital media's connectivity.

My findings about the deficiencies of digital media further explore how digital media limits our gospel workers' young adult ministries. Although the literature displays that digital media can result in issues such as overuse, distraction, shallow interaction, and avoidance of in-person communication, the biggest issue Adventist workers face is a lack of in-person communication and human touch. This, in particular, interferes with the workers' core task in the mission field: communicating gospel messages to their friends through trustworthy relationships.

My findings about relationship-building processes and spiritual interaction relate to my review of the literature in chapter 2, which looked at how attitudes and values of the younger generation as well as general trust-building factors affect relationships. However, the literature could not offer specific factors or cases showing what can stimulate personal interests and build trustworthiness in the relationship-building process between Adventist workers and non-Christian young adults. These findings suggest that learning new skills and joining in helpful activities allow non-Christian young adults to build relationships with Adventist workers.

The findings further defined trust-building factors that contribute to the deepening of relationships, such as benevolence, integrity, the pursuit of common goals, and secondhand information from credible friends. For example, in the context of my research, the findings specify two key elements of integrity: vulnerability and discretion. When Adventist workers exhibit their weaknesses to their non-Christian friends, and when they maintain confidentiality when trusted with their friends' inner issues, such behaviors demonstrate integrity.

My findings also necessitate digital media model practices that can boost positive aspects and mitigate limitations of digital media for building relationships. Those principles enable Adventist workers to use digital media more strategically and intentionally for deepening relationships of trust and dialogue and sharing the gospel with their non-Christian young

Part Two: Field Research

adult friends. Next, in order to discover the most efficient way to identify digital media model practices and establish a change plan, I analyze the regional culture of the Middle East and North Africa and that of my organization, Middle East and North Africa Union Mission of Seventh-day Adventists, as my leadership context.

Part Three

Application

The analysis of the data displayed that digital media is embedded into Adventist workers' relationship building and spiritual interactions with non-Christian young adults in the Middle East and North Africa. Based on the findings, in part III, I outline the process of identifying digital media practices and demonstrate how the Middle East and North Africa Union Mission of Seventh-day Adventists can apply those findings to equip its frontline workers for relationship building and spiritual interaction with non-Christian young adults.

In chapter 7, I describe the process of the pilot brainstorming group activities and outcomes from the pilot. I also demonstrate how I will apply my findings to a larger group of Adventist workers. In chapter 8, I conclude this dissertation by identifying additional gaps for future research in order to add to the field of missiology and advance the kingdom of God with non-Christian young adults in the Middle East and North Africa.

7

Application Strategy

My analysis of the field research data demonstrated that digital communication media (DCM) plays crucial roles in deepening relationships of trust and allowing for spiritual interactions between Adventist frontline workers and their non-Christians young adult friends. First, DCM catalyzes interactions following an initial spontaneous in-person encounter. Second, it fosters a sense of care and togetherness between Adventist workers and non-Christian young adults, which enables Adventist workers to establish trust. Finally, DCM provides platforms and security for spiritual interaction. In my field research, I also observed the limitations of DCM, including that it is highly time-consuming, can result in superficial interactions, and contributes to insufficient human touch. My field research observations indicate that DCM is embedded in Adventist workers' in-field ministries for young adults, whether or not the workers recognize the influence.

In response to my conclusions based on these observations, I intend the focus for my change project to be finding principles to boost the effective utilization of DCM for Adventist workers in the Middle East and North Africa (MENA). These principles can be implemented to enhance Adventist workers' relationship building and spiritual interaction with their non-Christian young adult friends. In this chapter, first, I report on the group brainstorming activities I conducted as my pilot project to co-create DCM model practices with frontline workers. Second, I describe the plans I hope to enact for the Middle East and North Africa Union Mission of the Seventh-day Adventists (MENAUM) to bring about long-term change related to my pilot project. I then offer a conclusion explaining what insights this pilot project provided for my research and for the future change process.

PILOT IMPLEMENTATION AND OUTCOMES

I have endeavored to answer my application question: "What digital media practices can be identified to strengthen Adventist frontline workers' relationship building and spiritual interactions with young adult non-Christians?" To this end, I conducted group brainstorming activities with four Adventist frontline workers who represent different fields and regions—sub-entities of MENAUM—to co-create DCM model practices. I utilized the online communication platform Zoom and instant messengers for the brainstorming sessions in July and August 2021.

Choice of Pilot Method

My field research findings indicate that DCM significantly impacts Adventist workers' in-field ministries for their young adult friends. However, during the interviews, I noticed that several gospel workers had not considered the meaningful connection between DCM and their relationship building and spiritual interaction with their non-Christian friends. I thus attempted to pilot a project that can enhance the use of DCM for Adventist workers' in-field ministries.

I expect that members and workers within MENAUM may respect a group approach for creating and implementing DCM practices if they are encouraged to participate in the process, which would foster a collaborative spirit in seeking collective wisdom. By participating in this group activity, the frontline workers can feel that they are the co-creators and main actors to develop ideas and visions for their fellow gospel workers' thriving ministries.

The intents I list below provide criteria and insights for my pilot method:

1. The pilot method should be participatory in horizontal communication.
2. The pilot method should be collaborative in seeking collective wisdom.
3. The pilot method should affirm and recognize frontline workers as experienced partners in fostering grassroots coordination.

Application Strategy

4. The pilot method should focus on creating DCM model practices based on my findings as a component of the potential change, which can benefit frontline workers in different fields and regions.
5. The pilot method should increase buy-in from the participants and other frontline workers within MENAUM for the change.

Based on these criteria, I chose to pilot a brainstorming group with frontline workers.

Context of the Group Brainstorming Activities

In the light of reasoning and planning as I described above, I formed a brainstorming group consisting of four frontline workers from fields and regions of MENAUM who actively utilize DCM in their young adult ministries. I attempted to design the group activities to recognize them as partners and to co-create DCM model practices as the first step of the anticipated long-term change. To this end, I went through a four-step process: (1) identifying and inviting participants, (2) sharing research findings, (3) co-creating DCM model practices based on findings, and (4) receiving feedback and adjustment.

IDENTIFYING AND INVITING PARTICIPANTS

Since Adventist frontline workers were my primary focus for the group brainstorming activity, identifying prospective participants among frontline workers for the group was the first step of the process. I attempted to identify frontline workers who fit the criteria for "early adopters," as introduced by respected communication theorist and sociologist Everett M. Rogers. Rogers explains that because they are influential and other members look to them as examples, "this adopter category is generally sought by change agents as a local missionary for speeding the diffusion process."[1] While these individuals can prompt change by adopting innovations earlier than do other average members, early adopters are not more advanced than the average members of a system.[2]

Based on this description of early adopters as well as my field research, committee participation, and personal interactions with frontline workers, I endeavored to identify frontline workers who fit the following criteria:

---

1. Rogers, *Diffusion of Innovations*, 386.
2. Rogers, *Diffusion of Innovations*, 386.

Part Three: Application

1. Frontline workers who actively utilize DCM in their relationship-building processes and spiritual interactions with non-Christian young adults in the field. Because of their contribution, other workers are more likely to have confidence in the co-created DCM practices.

2. Frontline workers who have been presented by ministry leaders at the various committees as role models due to their exemplary in-field ministries. This will allow the co-created DCM practices to impact the frontline workers' peers and administrators.

3. Frontline workers whose in-field activities I am familiar with because of our previous personal interactions. They have preestablished relationships with me, so they can more deeply and freely express their opinions.

4. Frontline workers who represent different sub-entities—fields and regions—of MENAUM. As a result of the participation of these individuals, DCM practices can have broader applications for workers in various fields and regions in MENAUM.

On May 20, 2021, I contacted each prospective participant by phone to explain the group brainstorming process in order to obtain verbal intention of participation. Four gospel workers who work in different locations expressed their willingness to participate in the group. ADV-1[3](male) and ADV-2 (female) work in Northeast and West African countries in the continent's northernmost part. ADV-3 (female) and ADV-4 (male) work in the western Asian countries in the Middle East. Limiting the number of participants to this number allowed each of the participants greater opportunity for contribution.

Sharing Research Findings

For the second step of the pilot, I gave a lecture on my field research findings to the four participants in a group meeting held on July 7, 2021 (see appendix D). I utilized the online communication platform Zoom for this meeting. If I had held the project group meeting in person, it would have required considerable time and travel costs. Also, the added complication of COVID-19 travel restrictions could have been a major obstacle. Zoom

---

3. In order to preserve the anonymity of participants for security reasons in the region, I refer to each by a code rather than by name.

communication circumvented any travel challenges due to COVID-19 and allowed for security.

I had three intents for this process:

1. I intended that through the lecture on my findings, the participants would understand the impact of digital media on relationship development and spiritual interactions according to the framework of key themes.
2. I intended that the participants would have opportunities to verify my field research findings based on their experiences and perspectives.
3. I intended to lay the foundations of the tangible DCM model practices that the participants will develop.

The length of this group activity was about ninety minutes. The meeting consisted of four segments. First, I made a presentation about my research findings. Second, the participants asked questions and offered feedback on the findings. Third, the participants suggested rough ideas about DCM model practices. Finally, I informed participants of the process of the next activity: co-creating DCM model practices.

Co-creation of DCM Model Practices

After the first group brainstorming activity, I distributed a template document that displayed topical categories based on my lecture on findings to help participants brainstorm about DCM practices (see appendix E). Using that template, each participant could develop best practices based on my research findings that would boost the relationship-building process and spiritual interaction with MENA young adults. This method also allowed participants to spend a couple of weeks pondering and sharpening their ideas and principles before offering their suggestions.

Upon completion of the initial draft, throughout July and August, I held a brainstorming session with each participant via Zoom, phone call, or instant messenger applications so the participants could clarify and supplement the written information. Throughout the process, I offered feedback on their suggestions. The average length of each brainstorming session for the co-creation of best DCM practices was approximately forty minutes.

Part Three: Application

FINAL FEEDBACK AND ADJUSTMENT

After the third step—co-creation of DCM practices with each participant—I integrated all the principles into one document. I then sent the draft of DCM model practices to the four participants and asked them to review, confirm, or recommend revisions as well as provide additional insights.

This process enabled the participants and me to revisit and reconfirm the suggested ideas. Based on their feedback, I polished the document to achieve the goal of this study: to determine what digital media practices can be identified to strengthen Adventist frontline workers' relationship building and spiritual interactions with young adult non-Christians.

Group Brainstorming Activities

Building on the brief description of the brainstorming process above, in this section, I provide information on how I implemented group brainstorming activities. I also explain how the content of the group activities relates to my research findings and to frontline workers in the Middle East and North Africa.

INVITATION

After identifying prospective participants among frontline workers, I contacted each Adventist worker to explain that they were invited to the meeting as participants. The invitation allowed me to acknowledge their experience and knowledge. In a similar vein, I strove to reveal possible outcomes of the meeting to the participants during our initial communication. For example, I told them that although I conducted the field research and analyzed the research data, the frontline workers who live and work in the field can advance the findings as concrete DCM model practices for helping other frontline workers. I also explained that their understanding and perspectives are critical both for my research and for the change process. The opportunities and practical applications I described increased the workers' engagement in the brainstorming group. When I extended the invitation to participate in the pilot program, my invitation set the tone for recognition and horizontal communication; as a result, the prospective participants expressed their active willingness to join the group.

Application Strategy

SHARING RESEARCH FINDINGS: LECTURE ON FINDINGS

One of the key purposes of me giving a lecture on my findings was to enable the participants to understand systematically the impact of digital media on in-field ministries. For example, thematic keywords from my findings can concretely express participants' vague ideas or experiences about the impact of digital media on their ministries. Another aim was to lay foundations for the participants to advance my findings to model practices by offering them insights and a framework from my research. I also expected that the participants would verify my field research findings. To these ends, I conducted a lecture on my findings for the participants (see appendix D).

Overall, all the participants supported the key findings: DCM (1) catalyzes interactions; (2) creates a sense of care and togetherness; (3) provides platforms and security for spiritual interaction; (4) has limitations, such as time-consumption, shallow interactions, and lack of human touch; and (5) is embedded into Adventist workers' young adult ministries. One participant commented, "Things you have reported are almost the same with what I experience, and I believe that the phenomena happen not only in my field but also in other MENA territories" (ADV-1). Another worker noted, "Your conclusions are pretty much what we experience in the field" (ADV-4), which confirmed that my findings reflected their general experiences in tangible and systematic structures.

They also linked specific findings to their ministry practices. For example, in response to finding that in-person and digital communication are supplementary for relationship development and spiritual interactions, one worker noted, "Digital media provides us with opportunities to nurture our friends before and after face-to-face meetings" (ADV-4). As the participants reflected the findings in the light of their experience, they expressed the realization that digital media has become an integral part of their in-field ministries for non-Christian young adults.

Further, the lecture stimulated the participants to give shape to the findings. One of the key findings in the lecture was that continuous and regular digital communication increases a sense of connectedness and togetherness (see appendix D). This finding enabled the participants to suggest tentative ideas of the time and frequency for digital communication that can impact the depth of relationships with their non-Christian young adult friends. As the participants attempted to advance my findings to specific principles, I introduced the idea of co-creating best DCM practices. They affirmed the necessity of DCM model practices for other frontline workers.

In summary, through the lecture on findings, the brainstorming group understood how digital media has been integrated with their relationship development and spiritual interactions with non-Christian young adults. My lecture on findings also allowed them to develop tentative ideas of utilizing digital media for deepening relationships of trust and dialogue. The participants validated my research findings and conclusions, and they affirmed the necessity of DCM model practices.

Co-creation of DCM Models: Finding Bright Spots

To allow the participants to fully express their ideas based on my findings, I suggested they take the time to write down their thoughts and opinions before our one-on-one interactions. In doing so, they could reflect on the lecture on findings and concretize their thoughts about DCM prior to individual meetings with me. To achieve this, after the lecture on July 7, 2021, I shared with the participants via encrypted group chat a template document designed to guide the participants to advance my findings to specific principles (see appendix E). The primary function of the template document was to provide a framework aligned with my field research findings to assist the participants' reflection process. For example, my field research focused on three areas regarding DCM: (1) the impact of DCM on relationship building, (2) the impact of DCM on spiritual interaction, and (3) limitations of DCM on young adult ministry. The template document enabled the participants to categorize their suggestions into those areas based on my lecture on findings.

The participants and I agreed on a two-week time frame to complete the template document. Each sent me the document directly, through encrypted instant messenger or encrypted email service, within the two-week time period. I then communicated with each one individually through encrypted phone calls and text messages in order to guide them to sharpen their ideas and suggestions in tune with my findings. Several insightful themes emerged from the individual consultation meetings.

Openness and Genuineness

My field research indicated that openness and genuineness were critical elements for Adventist workers to build relationships with their non-Christian

Application Strategy

friends. In line with this, the brainstorming group mentioned that these are vital values when frontline workers interact with their young friends on DCM. One participant shared,

> Be honest about who you are—within [security] reason—when you post to social media. Don't try to hide things they may not agree with. . . . Many times, these open the door for questions about who you are and how you think, which in turn provides you a chance to reciprocate and ask them questions. (ADV-3)

In a similar vein, another participant commented, "Don't try to be perfect on the media [DCM]. When you show your weaknesses, your friends are more likely open toward you" (ADV-4). These suggest that Adventist workers' open and genuine attitudes on DCM may deepen their relationships of trust with their friends.

A male worker from a northeast African country emphasized the importance that Adventist workers maintain a nonjudgmental mindset when they use DCM. He shared his experience:

> I would advise our workers to remove their own assumptions and judgments about their non-Christian friends on DCM. The media is there to form friendships with them by exploring and discovering. Even if they don't seem to be interested in spiritual stuff, you will be surprised at how many of them approach you about spiritual topics later. (ADV-1)

His experience indicates that when Adventist workers seek to connect with their friends through DCM, they need to be open to the unexpected.

Strategic Intention

My findings and my reflections demonstrated that Adventist workers' use of digital media with missional intention is key to catalyzing relationships and spiritual interactions. Building on this, the participants recommended that in order to maximize DCM's effectiveness for deepening relationships of dialogue, Adventist workers must be strategically intentional when they use the media. For example, one participant encouraged Adventist workers to join various groups on Facebook or WhatsApp in order to find non-Christian friends who share similar interests. This participant also proposed that Adventist workers must understand the primary role of DCM in their own young adult ministry contexts. For instance, while one Adventist

Part Three: Application

worker may focus on utilizing DCM to create more opportunities for face-to-face meetings, another can employ the media to share content for online interactions. The participant commented, "You need to make a personal strategy, considering your ministry needs" (ADV-2).

Another worker explained that he already anticipates certain topics, reactions, and questions when he shares content (such as news articles) with his non-Christian friends on DCM. He stated, "In doing so, we can openly share our thoughts and views on various subjects as Christians. We should be very intentional" (ADV-1). This statement reveals the need to pursue Adventist workers' strategic views of their use of DCM for enhancing their relationships with non-Christian young adults.

Complementary Effect

My field research findings showed that DCM and in-person communication (IPC) complement each other for Adventist workers' young adult ministries in the field. Based on the findings, the participants recommended that Adventist workers need to utilize both digital and in-person communication for effective in-field ministry. One participant commented, "If possible, find ways to balance between face-to-face interactions and digital communications" (ADV-3). She explained that workers need to make time for both. Another Adventist worker supported this point: "We need to remember that DCM is super important to relate to our young adult friends—and the magic also happens in face-to-face" (ADV-4).

As a practical example and suggestion, one participant explained how she utilized both DCM and IPC with her non-Christian friends: "Let's say that you were talking about the Bible with your friend in person, but you couldn't finish the conversation for whatever reasons. Then, you follow up the topic on DCM and share related materials with your friend" (ADV-2). In this case, she employed DCM to supplement the incomplete face-to-face communication. The worker also described the opposite case: "If you started a spiritual conversation on DCM and your friend didn't understand what you said enough, you set a time and place where you can discuss the topic face-to-face and clarify everything" (ADV-2). In this case, IPC complements the unfinished digital communication.

Similarly, another worker described the effectiveness of digital communication for face-to-face interaction. He observed, "DCM helped me and my friends to learn about each other and build a strong sense of connection in a distance. When we met in person after months of [COVID-19] lockdown, we already learned much about each other" (ADV-1). The above statements from the participants indicate that Adventist workers need to utilize strengths of both DCM and IPC.

Regular Communication

During the lecture I gave on my findings, I demonstrated the importance of continual digital communication to deepen relationships of trust and catalyze spiritual interactions by creating a sense of togetherness. Building upon this point, the participants recommended that Adventist workers' relationship building could be more effective if they were to use DCM regularly. One participant explained, "If you use DCM thirty minutes every day for your friends, you can connect with around three friends by checking on them and a small talk, and that still provides a sense of connection" (ADV-1). Another worker suggested that even simple DCM communication could be helpful. She commented, "Take time to connect regularly. It can be as simple as a reaction to something they post, or a short text saying hi or wishing them a good day" (ADV-3). These statements not only confirm my field research data that indicated that checking on others was crucial for creating a sense of care, but they also suggest practical methods.

Another worker supported the idea of regular DCM communication, but she emphasized that it is vital to do so on a schedule that works for the Adventist workers' non-Christian friends. She described, "When I text with my friends, I do that in the late evening night, because most of my friends are available for texting" (ADV-2). She also explained the benefit of regularly calling friends using instant messenger applications: "At least twice a week, call your three closest friends using WhatsApp or Telegram. Ask how they are doing and listen to them. They will open their hearts, and you will understand them better" (ADV-2). These points indicate that regular digital communication can help Adventist workers deepen relationships with their young adult friends.

Expressiveness

The lecture I gave on my findings described how digital media entails mutual interactions in expressiveness. Upon hearing this, the brainstorming group proposed that Adventist workers must be expressive in their digital media

Part Three: Application

communications. One worker observed, "Relationship grows by giving your small expressions—such as likes and comments—to your friends on DCM" (ADV-4). He advised that Adventist workers need to make sure that they are connected via DCM with their friends whom they encounter in person. In support of this, another participant stated the importance of being reactive: "Respond when they comment on what you post; this lets them know you appreciate their own attempts at connecting" (ADV-3).

Another worker shared her similar opinion:

> After the first encounter, send a message to your new friend and tell her that you enjoyed the time together and ask when she would meet again. This kind of text message is important because it shows your willingness to build friendship. (ADV-2)

The participant also explained that using emojis to express to her female friends her emotional values of care and compassion was helpful to build and deepen the relationships of trust and dialogue. Such emojis provide a visualization of intangible feelings, which was critical for young adult friends in the region.

Diverse Topics and Casual Mannerisms

According to my findings, digital media provides various talking points for conversations between Adventist workers and their non-Christian young adults. The findings also showed that the act of casually asking after friends on digital media can be effective to deepen relationships. Based on these findings, some participants mentioned the necessity of a casual tone and mannerisms when Adventist workers interact with their non-Christian friends. One stated that workers can use DCM to display a different picture of Christianity and Christians, and sometimes Adventist workers need to demonstrate a good sense of humor for their friends (ADV-1). In line with this, another worker commented,

> Not everything has to be spiritually focused. At the end, they're the same as any friend. Friendships grow best naturally as people connect across multiple areas of interest and through many topics. If you focus just on the goal of getting to spirituality, you will miss many opportunities. (ADV-3)

Comments such as the above indicate that although Adventist workers' ultimate ministry goal is to introduce the gospel to their non-Christian

Application Strategy

friends, they should be open to opportunities to engage around other topics on DCM. Likewise, Adventist workers need to be fluent in the language of a light and casual mood.

Patience

In the lecture on my findings, I showcased that when Adventist workers and their non-Christian friends engage in conversations on sensitive issues or topics, digital communication can offer a buffer that protects their relationships. Digital media offers young adult friends time and freedom to ponder and respond when they want. Based on this finding, the brainstorming group suggested that digital communication requires patience from Adventist workers when they interact with their young adult friends. One participant encouraged Adventist workers not to expect active reactions or participation from their friends on DCM all the time. He observed,

> It is easy for people who love to argue and discuss to express themselves in whatever circumstances. There are also people who can't do it easily. In my experience, DCM helps those shy people question and answer in private. However, you should wait until they respond to you instead of pushing for immediate reaction. (ADV-1)

This shows the flexibility of DCM: people can choose when to react or not react to questions and comments. To maximize the strength of DCM, Adventist workers should respect periods of silence from their friends on DCM.

Habit of Sharing

According to my findings, digital media provides Adventist workers opportunities for spiritual interactions by allowing them to share spiritual content more easily than they can in offline communication. Based on this finding, the brainstorming group argued that the habit of sharing is a critical DCM practice for Adventist workers' in-field ministry. One worker stated that he could ignite productive and meaningful conversation with his non-Christian young adult friends by sharing funny videos on DCM (ADV-4). Concurring with this, another participant explained that sharing songs often provides her with various opportunities for deep spiritual dialogue with friends (ADV-2).

Part Three: Application

Another participant stated, "We can openly share our opinions about certain subjects by sharing social media content. Sharing something on DCM seems to be an insignificant act, but with right intention, it can bring about much more than you think" (ADV-1). One worker shared a specific experience of this:

> You initiate spiritual interaction by sharing spiritual content. They are interested in what you post, as this provides a starting point for talking. During COVID-19, we posted daily nature photos with Bible verses that they commented on with voice notes. (ADV-3)

The above comments demonstrate how the habit of sharing on DCM can ignite meaningful spiritual interactions between Adventist workers and their young adult friends.

Habit of Asking Questions

According to my findings, non-Christian young adults' questions on life issues and religion offer Adventist workers opportunities to deepen relationships of trust and spiritual interactions. In response to this finding, the brainstorming group suggested that not only is answering the questions important, but also the habit of asking non-Christians questions on digital media can be critical. The participants argued that the habit of asking questions should be a key DCM practice to enhance Adventist workers' deepening relationships of trust and dialogue with their young adult friends. One worker suggested that when workers notice topics on DCM that they don't understand, they must ask their non-Christian friends for help navigating these aspects of local culture and language. He stated, "They love to help, and they tend to trust you more when they can help you somehow" (ADV-4). In line with this, another participant explained why questions help build trust between Adventist workers and young adult friends. He observed, "We should try to ask more questions on DCM, because the act shows that we are willing to learn from our friends" (ADV-1). This observation implies that asking questions via DCM is a sign of a humble attitude.

At the same time, one worker emphasized the importance of asking spiritual questions. She commented, "Don't hesitate to ask spiritual questions on DCM. They will surely answer, and you can have long discussions about your questions" (ADV-2). This experience shows that the habit of asking questions via DCM can naturally lead Adventist workers

Application Strategy

to meaningful relationships of trust and spiritual interactions with their young adult friends.

PAYING ATTENTION TO SMALL THINGS

My lecture on the findings demonstrated how digital media allows Adventist workers to observe their non-Christian friends' moods and life events. Based on this finding, the brainstorming group suggested that Adventist workers need to be observant of their young adult friends on DCM. One participant endeavored to discover interests he and his non-Christian friends shared by paying attention to their DCM. In this way, he was able to invite his friends into relevant conversations and to events that interested them (ADV-4). In support of this idea, another worker mentioned,

> This is the time to be detail oriented. Remember things they've mentioned or posted and check in later to ask about it. Notice the small things that convey their mood or what is going on in their life at that time—where their thoughts are. (ADV-3)

Another participant also asserted the importance of paying attention to small things on DCM in order to build trust. He noted,

> Looks like my local friends are much more sensitive to small expressions and gestures than my friends in the West. So you should show that you care about even insignificant-looking matters—such as asking about their meals—by utilizing simple interaction on DCM. It will show that you consider the person as a friend. (ADV-1)

The group recommended that Adventist workers can build and deepen relationship with their non-Christian friends by observing and expressing insignificant topics through DCM.

AUDACITY FOR SPIRITUAL INTERACTION

The brainstorming group emphasized that a courageous attitude on DCM can catalyze spiritual interaction with friends. My field research data already indicated that spirituality is embedded into the social life of young adults in the region, so talking about religion and spiritual issues is mundane. In line with this finding, one participant suggested that Adventist workers need to look for safe opportunities to discuss spiritual issues on DCM. He observed, "For example, we can ask our friends about the meaning of

Part Three: Application

religious holidays on DCM. That may enable us to connect the topic with the gospel" (ADV-1). Another worker commented,

> Posting and commenting with spiritual thoughts [on DCM] is perfectly normal in the non-Christian context in this region. They themselves have so many words to explain the character of God, and they invoke them for every circumstance, both good and bad. Using this same tactic back toward them is familiar, but you can take it a step further by adding a story or Bible verse that conveys the name of God they are needing in their problem. (ADV-3)

In a similar vein, she asserted, "Don't be afraid of WhatsApp groups where several Muslims know each other. They can spiritually interact with you" (ADV-3). These points suggest that Adventist workers should courageously initiate spiritual interactions on DCM.

One worker explained the necessity of praying with non-Christian friends on DCM. She mentioned, "A marvelous way to show care for them, it is praying. Listen and then pray with them through DCM is easy because nobody is seeing" (ADV-2). Another participant encouraged, "Let them know you are praying for their specific situation and invite them to pray as well. Celebrate together God's answers when they come" (ADV-4). My field research data showed that prayer was one of the top topics that provide Adventist workers with opportunities for spiritual interaction. To reinforce this, the participants stated that Adventist workers need to utilize DCM boldly for their prayer ministries.

Diverse Platforms

Although the lecture did not deal with specific digital media platforms, in the process of the brainstorming group activity, my findings enabled the participants to develop ideas of digital platforms. The participants suggested that Adventist workers should utilize different digital communication platforms to deal with diverse situations. For example, one female worker mentioned the effectiveness of the Zoom video conference application: "If you already have a group of friends with common interests and matured friendship, you can create a Zoom group to teach them something new and share Bible stories with them" (ADV-2). Another worker stated the opposite. He explained, "Introverts are not comfortable with Zoom conference calls. They are easily neglected in the group setting. In this case, texting on an instant messenger application will be a better option" (ADV-1). These

Application Strategy

points suggest that Adventist workers should understand the right format and platform of digital communication for different circumstances and different individuals to facilitate deepening relationships.

Following my lecture on findings, the brainstorming group suggested attitudes and practices that can maximize the effectiveness of digital media to deepen relationships of trust and dialogue. Based upon my findings, the lecture, and the brainstorming session, I developed eleven best DCM practices for Adventist workers in MENA.

Best DCM Practices

One of the main purposes of this group brainstorming activity was the co-creation of best DCM practices to deepen Adventist workers' relationships of trust and dialogue with their non-Christian young adult friends. During the brainstorming, I was able to discover several bright spots for Adventist workers' best DCM practices. As an outcome of the co-creating activity, based on those spots, I suggest eleven best DCM practices.

1. *Be open*: Be honest about who you are—within the bounds of appropriate security practices—when you communicate with your friends on DCM. Don't try to hide things with which they may not agree. Several frontline workers witnessed that this transparency often can open a door for questions about who you are and how you think, which in turn provides you a chance to reciprocate and ask them questions.

2. *Be vulnerable*: Do not try to be perfect on DCM. When you show that you are also an ordinary human who experiences frustration and anxiety, your non-Christian friends are more likely to be open with you. This vulnerability can increase the quality of relationships between Adventist workers and young adults.

3. *Be intentional*: Join a group where you can interact with non-Christian young adults with whom you share similar interests. Anticipate possible reactions and discussions when you share specific content, so choose your topic before you share. Choose your DCM platform strategically. For instance, once you have an established relationship, a video conference call will offer you and your friends diverse ways of interaction. If you interact with introverts, text messages can be more effective than video calls. It is most effective to have a DCM strategy designed specifically for your ministry context. You need to define

Part Three: Application

the best uses of DCM for your ministry needs, such as in initiating conversations and/or in-person meetings.

4. *Utilize both DCM and IPC to complement each other*: After an in-person spiritual interaction with a friend, do not wait until the next meeting. Follow up the topic on DCM to retain his or her interest as well as a sense of connection. Likewise, you need to initiate face-to-face interactions between digital communications. This strategy can catalyze deepening relationships of trust and dialogue with non-Christian young adults.

5. *Be a regular communicator*: Regularly communicate with non-Christian friends on DCM. Frontline workers experienced that regularly checking in on their young friends was crucial to create a sense of care and connectedness. Even spending as little as ten to thirty minutes on this helps to deepen relationships of trust and dialogue.

6. *Be reactive*: Frontline workers observed that simple responses and reactions on DCM such as likes, comments, and emojis were effective to show care and compassion for non-Christian friends. These indications of care help deepening relationships of trust and dialogue among Adventist workers and young adults.

7. *Keep sharing and questioning*: Frontline workers emphasized the importance of sharing and questioning on DCM. Sharing casual, social, and spiritual content with non-Christian friends can bring various opportunities to deepen relationships and initiate spiritual conversations. Likewise, asking non-Christian friends social, cultural, and spiritual questions can help build reciprocal trust.

8. *Be patient*: A lack of an active response from non-Christian friends on DCM should not be a cause for disappointment. Introverts often need more time to express their thoughts than do extroverts. Individuals need different amounts of time to find the right opportunity and place (or platform) to share their opinions.

9. *Understand the power of small things*: As relationships grow, pay attention on DCM to details of your friends' lives. Those small things can enable you to engage your friends in topics and opportunities that will allow for deepening relationships and spiritual growth.

10. *Don't be afraid of spiritual interactions*: You can find safe ways to initiate spiritual interactions with your friends, because spirituality

Application Strategy

is embedded into MENA societies, such as through religious rituals and artifacts. Therefore, expressing your spiritual thoughts on DCM is considered acceptable and normal, which can allow for opportunities for deeper spiritual interaction.

11. *Do a digital detox regularly*: Set hours or days on a regular basis that you can take a break from digital media and digital communications to prevent the negative effects of digital communication media that can harm your in-field ministries. Let your friends know your detox routine to avoid misunderstandings.

I anticipate four primary areas of change in the long-term future: (1) awareness, (2) best DCM practices, (3) DCM resources for sharing, and (4) the fostering of a culture of digital sharing. I anticipate that these eleven practices will inform the development of DCM resources that can be utilized for effectively practicing those best principles. At the same time, these principles and resources can be critical elements for fostering a culture of digital sharing.

When I asked the brainstorming group for their final feedback about these eleven best DCM practices, the group recommended that these practices be taught to both new and current workers. They also verified that because these practices were created by frontline workers from different fields and regions, they could be applied by Adventist workers in various locations.

I believe that through this pilot project, the participants and I took an important first step toward application of my research. In addition, this process confirmed my field research findings about the importance of DCM for Adventist workers' relationship building and spiritual interaction. Further steps in application can discover and develop a plan to utilize the best DCM practices to enhance Adventist workers' young adult ministries.

IMPLEMENTING A STRATEGY TO STRENGTHEN ADVENTIST WORKERS

Sharing my findings in the lecture followed by the group brainstorming activities led to the identification of digital media model practices. During the process, I endeavored to demonstrate my research findings, which stimulated the participants to progress the findings to model practices.

At the end of the meeting, when I asked the participants for their feedback, they stated that this type of process can be helpful for other

Part Three: Application

workers to discover the impact of digital media on their relationship building and spiritual interactions and to develop tailored DCM practices for enhancing their in-field ministries. To effectively apply my findings and digital media principles to a larger group of Adventist workers, I outline below the plans to run local brainstorming groups.

Obtaining Support from Leaders by Sharing Findings

The first step to involve in-field workers is to offer a presentation that will help MENAUM leadership and local leaders understand my research findings. My doing this will help them discover the roles of digital media in frontline workers' relationship development and spiritual interactions. This presentation will also increase awareness of the problems I discovered, such as Adventist workers' dichotomous views on DCM and the lack of a frontline strategy despite the impact of media.

Based on this understanding, the leaders may support the necessity of local brainstorming groups to enhance Adventist workers' in-field ministries. I can speak to those on the presidential council and mission committees. Through these, I hope to obtain momentum and permission to work with frontline workers.

Identifying and Inviting Field and Region Workers

Upon the approval of the leadership team, I will identify three frontline workers for each field and region (sub-entities of MENAUM)—fifteen in total—who can fit the role of early adopters and who, in the future, can lead brainstorming sessions with their fellow frontline workers. When I invite them, I will inform them of the purpose of the brainstorming groups in which they will participate. I will also share my intention that they become facilitators of similar groups in the future; this will increase buy-in and ensure their active attention and participation.

Based on their agreement to participate, I will schedule three-day training sessions in Lebanon, where the regional church headquarters are located. By doing so, I can avoid any security and safety concerns, since participants will engage in the brainstorming and training sessions outside of their mission fields.

Application Strategy

Day One: Sharing Research Findings with Selected Frontline Workers

The first session will involve me giving a lecture on my research findings. Through this lecture, I will provide insights and a framework of the findings, which will stimulate participants' ideas, as I experienced in the pilot brainstorming group. To this end, I will also facilitate a Q&A session after the lecture for clarifying and elaborating on the findings. This can encourage the participants to reflect and offer feedback.

After the lecture and Q&A session, I will distribute my lecture notes and the template document for DCM model practices. The participants will use the lecture notes to review my findings, and they will be able to share them with other workers in the future. The template document is designed to help participants develop their own ideas of digital media model practices based on my findings. The participants will be asked to prepare two presentations for the next day. First, for practice, each participant will present my research findings along with their reflections. Next, based on the findings, each participant will demonstrate tailored DCM model practices that can impact his or her young adult ministry.

Day Two: Facilitating, Coaching, and Creating

As each participant presents the research findings with their reflections, this activity will equip them with the ability to present the findings to other workers when they facilitate local brainstorming groups. Their reflections can also reveal how the findings may or may not be relevant to their contexts.

Following the lectures, the participants will present their ideas of best DCM practices based on the findings. While each one presents, I will guide other participants to write down their reflections on each point rather than instantly expressing their thoughts. Immediate negative reactions can hinder active idea formation and brainstorming at an initial stage. Asking participants to wait to comment can encourage everyone to bring ideas—even unripe ones—that can be developed further during the group brainstorming process.

Upon the completion of each presentation, I will encourage everyone to offer feedback. The most important rule during this segment is that the person offering feedback must make suggestions that advance the original ideas rather than merely commenting on them. This process will allow the

Part Three: Application

participants to develop ideas together. After this, I will guide the participants to synthesize and polish the practices as a complete list. In addition, the workers must debrief about what they learned during the process and what they can improve when they facilitate local brainstorming sessions.

Day Three: Producing a List of Necessary Resources

I will facilitate another brainstorming session to create a list of resources in line with the best DCM practices that the participants produced through the brainstorming sessions on the second day. For example, if the brainstorming group recommended sharing news articles that can initiate spiritual interactions with non-Christian young adults, the list of selected news stories along with keywords and hyperlinks can catalyze the practice. To this end, the participants can create a potential list of digital resources.

I can then outline the previous steps of the brainstorming group activities as a model process, which will enable the participants to hold regional brainstorming sessions with their coworkers to co-create best DCM practices and a list of digital resources. Since three representatives from each field and region will participate in the training, three brainstorming groups can be organized in each field and region—fifteen brainstorming groups in total.

Follow-Up

Each field and region usually holds an annual workers' training and meeting. I recommend the local leaders allow the trained facilitators from their fields and regions to organize and conduct brainstorming group activities during the annual meetings. During the local brainstorming group activities, based on my research findings, all workers within MENAUM territories can discover the integral roles of digital media in their relationship development and spiritual interactions with non-Christian young adults. In addition, they can progress the findings to DCM model practices relevant to their ministry contexts, which they can then exercise daily. Finally, they can also identify digital resources they can utilize in order to catalyze deepening relationships of trust and dialogue. In addition, I will form a task force consisting of media professionals within MENAUM to provide frontline workers with technical support for producing necessary digital resources, such as graphics, videos, and audios.

Application Strategy

Before the meetings, I will constantly communicate with those fifteen facilitators to guide and support them. Afterward, with each facilitator, I will review the documents that result from the local group brainstorming activities. At this stage, the most important action is to advise facilitators to continue to interact with their brainstorming group participants about how they exercise the model practices they produced based on the research findings. In order to inspire other workers, I also will ask each local brainstorming group to recommend one worker who can present his or her experience of exercising the model practices during quarterly MENAUM workers' trainings session.

SUMMARY

In this chapter, I briefly described why I chose the group brainstorming model for my pilot. I then illustrated the process of the pilot brainstorming group project. I also reported how the brainstorming activities were facilitated. Through the activities, the participants were able to discover the impact of digital media on their in-field ministries and create eleven best DCM practices based on my research finding.

Based on the pilot brainstorming group activities, I proposed ways to apply my research findings to a larger group of Adventist workers. I suggested three-day training sessions to prepare facilitators to conduct local brainstorming group activities and to follow up on the local participants.

8

Concluding Thoughts

My goal for this study was to discover how digital media affects Adventist frontline workers' relationship-building processes with non-Christian young adults. Through the achievement of this goal, based on my findings, I intended to identify digital media model practices that can deepen relationships by fostering trust and dialogue among Adventist workers and non-Christian young adults. With this original objective in mind, I conclude with a review of the dissertation's key findings, recommendations, and implications to fulfill the purpose of this study: enhancing Adventist workers' ministry of sharing God's redemptive love, grace, and peace with non-Christian young adults in the Middle East and North Africa (MENA) through online and offline relationships.

DISSERTATION REVIEW

In my role as the media ministries director for the Middle East and North Africa Union Mission of Seventh-day Adventists (MENAUM), I observed that digital media has certain functions in building and nurturing relationships with the younger generation in MENA. However, many Adventist workers and leaders have treated digital media as a mere tool for unilateral content distribution and evangelism. Although the Seventh-day Adventist Church acknowledges the usefulness of digital media for mission work, there has been a failure to address the influence of this technology on increasing the quality of relationships as part of the mission ecology in the MENA context. This drove the central issue of this study.

Concluding Thoughts

I embarked on an exploration of how communication patterns and social dynamics among Adventist workers and non-Christian young adults impact the deepening of relationships through trust and dialogue. Through my literature review, field research, and subsequent analysis, I endeavored to answer the following central questions:

1. What are communication patterns, involving digital media, among Adventist workers and non-Christian young adults?
2. What are social dynamics, focusing on relationship building, among Adventist workers and non-Christian young adults?
3. What are crucial elements for deepening relationships among Adventist workers and non-Christian young adults?

A review of the literature exhibited that communication patterns developed through the use of digital media have impacted relationships among individuals. Three sociality-related traits of digital media—open communication, connectivity, and interplay with real life—catalyze relationship development by increasing intimacy, continual connectedness, and the quality of real-world relationships. For example, digital media's trait of open communication based on anonymity or confidentiality can encourage users to share their innermost feelings with their friends via digital media, and that act enhances the quality of relationships by increasing intimacy.

The literature brought forth the fact that the social dynamics of the post-Arab Spring youths' attitudes and values in addition to general trust-building factors influenced relationship establishment. To deal with the issues of uncertainty and anxiety, Arab youth seek trustworthy relationships and autonomy from social and religious expectations. The literature also demonstrated that the deepening of trust in relationships is a collective activity between trustees and trusters; it is based on the characteristics of the trustee, common interests and goals, and the need for and benefits of taking risks. This review also revealed gaps in the literature: it did not provide sufficient information about communication patterns and social dynamics specifically for a missional context for Adventist workers and their non-Christian young adult friends. This gap necessitated localized field research.

My field research showed that digital media plays a significant role in building and deepening relationships among Adventist workers and non-Christian young adults in MENA. The research demonstrated that

Part Three: Application

care and self-disclosure, or openness, are critical elements to deepen trust and relationships. In this vein, digital media first catalyzes the process of learning about others and then creates a sense of care and togetherness as individuals continue to check on each other regularly without barriers of time and space. Digital media allows Adventist workers and non-Christian young adults to engage in deep spiritual conversations without security concerns and the risk of ruining relationships. Finally, the research showed that digital and in-person communication supplement each other to deepen relationships through trust and dialogue.

After discussing key findings in the light of the literature review, I concluded that this review is relevant to the findings and that my field research advanced the theories in the review. I also reviewed the primary findings in the light of application. I thus demonstrated major implications of the findings for digital media model practices. First, digital media model practices may display appropriate postures when workers use the technology in the relationship-building process. Second, digital media model practices can exhibit tangible methods and tips to maximize experiences of care and togetherness for deepening relationships of trust and dialogue among Adventist workers and non-Christian young adult friends. For example, by privately sharing relevant materials on digital media, Adventist workers can safely answer their non-Christian friends' sensitive religious questions. In doing so, Adventist workers can avoid direct confrontation but still discuss the topics through the use of digital materials, such as video. Finally, digital media model practices may show ways to mitigate the limitations of digital media.

The primary intention of my research was to enhance Adventist workers' ministry of sharing God's redemptive love, grace, and peace with non-Christian young adults in MENA through online and offline relationships. To fulfill this purpose, I chose the group brainstorming model for my pilot project to identify digital media model practices based on my research findings. The pilot project model helped the participants discover the integral roles of digital media in their field ministries though the lecture on my findings, and it enabled them to progress the findings to best DCM practices through the brainstorming session.

Through group brainstorming, Adventist frontline workers and I were able to co-create eleven best digital media practices: (1) be open, (2) be vulnerable, (3) be intentional, (4) utilize both digital communication media (DCM) and in-person communication (IPC), (5) be a regular communicator,

(6) be reactive, (7) keep sharing and questioning, (8) be patient, (9) understand the power of small things, (10) don't be afraid of spiritual interactions, and (11) regularly take breaks from your digital devices.

To apply what I discovered from my research findings and the pilot project, I designed a three-day training followed by a group brainstorming session. The objective is to take this training to a larger group of Adventist workers for the purpose of enhancing their young adult ministries. The key point of the training is to develop facilitators to organize and conduct local brainstorming group activities to enable all workers to create tailored DCM model practices and exercise the principles. These suggestions will impact deepening relationships of trust and dialogue between Adventist workers and non-Christian young adults.

RECOMMENDATIONS FOR FURTHER RESEARCH

This research project raised the need for further research to enhance our mission work. Below, I note three areas for further study.

First, although I endeavored to include a large sample of frontline workers within the MENAUM territory, Adventist workers who serve in high-risk countries were excluded from this research. If the conditions were to become safe and security issues could be managed, further research in these countries would expand our understanding of the potential impact of digital media on deepening relationships of trust and dialogue.

Second, the focus of this study was to discover how digital media affects Adventist workers' relationship-building processes with non-Christian young adults. Attention will need to be given to how digital media impacts other aspects of young adult ministry, such as in the decision-making process, Bible study methods, and leadership development. This will be a useful question for further research to enhance Adventist workers' in-field ministries to non-Christian young adults in MENA.

Finally, this study included Adventist workers who have face-to-face—or real-life—offline relationships with non-Christian young adults. However, the COVID-19 pandemic has significantly increased opportunities for our members and workers to begin to build relationships fully online through digital media without face-to-face interactions. I have also observed that, for security reasons, many people in MENA prefer longer interactions with our workers to take place online. In this case, further research about how non-presence digital communication affects the relationship-building

Part Three: Application

process between Adventist workers and non-Christian young adults will be helpful to strengthen the missional praxis of MENAUM.

IMPLICATIONS FOR THE FIELD OF MISSIOLOGY

God created human beings with a desire for interacting, sharing, loving, and caring for others in relationship.[1] Being interconnected with God, humanity, and all of creation is one of the critical elements that enables humans to live in the image of God.[2] In line with this, Angela Gorrell describes how digital media must reflect Jesus's social relationship values of "belonging, wholeness, and relationship with God and others."[3] These theological reflections on the sociality of human beings are significant because they touch on the core uses of socializing digital media, such as in the deepening of relationships. Therefore, today, digital media is an important aspect of missional praxis for the Adventist Church and its frontline workers to share God's redemptive love and care with others.

My research brought to light two critical issues related to missiology in the MENA context. According to my research, the impact of digital media on deepening relationships of trust and dialogue among Adventist workers and non-Christians has not been adequately addressed in the light of missiology. Christians have viewed digital media as a useful tool for evangelism and content sharing;[4] however, the focus has not been on the quality of relationships developed through digital media, which critically affects the mission ecology. The field of missiology needs to consider the role of digital media in relationship and communication dynamics in mission and also to provide more focus and guidance to enhancing relationships of trust and dialogue among Christians and non-Christians.

The role of Adventist media ministries as a mission strategy and the future possibilities within the Adventist Church are also important issues. As an organization, the Adventist Church operates an official television and radio network and invests in digital evangelism, but there is currently no direct interplay between media ministries and frontline mission work. The field of missiology needs to ask the question how those media initiatives impact the missional praxis of frontline workers in

1. Myers, *Engaging Globalization*, 18.
2. Friesen, *Thy Kingdom Connected*, 19.
3. Gorrell, *Always On*, 90.
4. Cloete, "Living in a Digital Culture"; Sathyanesan, "Internet Evangelism"; Schultze, "Following Pilgrims into Cyberspace."

Concluding Thoughts

different locations—for example, through nurturing relationships and the discipleship process. This question can catalyze the integration of media ministries with in-field mission work.

CLOSING REMARKS

Viggo Søgaard explains that communicating God's message to others is God's Great Commission (Matt 28:18–20).[5] Communication is the act of proclaiming God's message by words and deeds, which means that not only are the messages important, but the messengers' actions are also vital for gospel communication. Messengers are an integral part of the gospel, as is seen in Jesus Christ's incarnation.[6] In this vein, deepening trust and dialogue in relationships is critical to communicate the gospel, because it increases trustworthiness of our frontline workers as messengers.

The word *Christian* is often met with suspicion and negative perceptions from non-Christians in MENA. The Christian identity is associated with imperialism, colonialism, hostility, and unlawfulness according to the regional history, such as what happened in the Crusades. In this context, building relationships with non-Christian young adults is important for our frontline workers. Our Arab young adults can experience God's redemptive love and care through these relationships with trustworthy Adventist friends.

Given this context, I strove to define the role of digital media and its influence on both Adventist workers and their non-Christian young adult friends. My research demonstrated that digital media contributes to deepening relationships of trust and dialogue by fostering a sense of care and togetherness. This answers my question about the role of digital media in mission—it is not merely for the efficiency of immediate content sharing and unilateral evangelism methods.

Andy Crouch suggests that digital technologies are valuable for Christians if they create connections and conversations with people whom Christians encounter in person,[7] and Ryan Bolger and Kutter Callaway state that Christian love and forgiveness can be expressed in digital spaces.[8]

---

5. Søgaard, *Research in Church and Mission*, 30.
6. Kraft, *Communicating Jesus' Way*, 15.
7. Crouch, *Tech-Wise Family*, 13.
8. Bolger and Callaway, *Techno-Sapiens in a Networked Era*, 3.

Part Three: Application

Ilia Delio envisions the ways in which future digital technologies will help individuals build communities and deepen relationships.[9]

I now understand the desirable roles of digital technology in mission as well as the practices that can maximize its impact on deepening relationships. I continue to hope that digital technology will be a place to express God's love, care, and forgiveness to young Middle Easterners and North Africans who seek eternal certainty and security.

---

9. Delio, "Religion and Posthuman Life," 15, 27.

Appendix A

Guides for Interview, Focus Group, and Survey

INTERVIEWS

1. What is your primary initiative or role in your field?
2. What is your age?
3. How many years have you served?
4. How have you been able to create the first contact with young adult friends?
5. How have you maintained your relationships with young adult friends?
6. What are the most important factors to establish close rapport with young adults?
7. How do you usually introduce spiritual topics to your young adult friends?
8. Have you noticed unique behaviors, cultures, or attitudes of young adults in virtual interaction that you do not notice in person?
9. How has digital communication media (DCM) influenced your life? (Positive and negative)
10. For what ministry task do you use DCM?
11. Personally, what do you think the positives and negatives are of DCM in young adult ministry or discipleship?
12. Are there things you can't do on DCM that you can do in person for young adult ministry or discipleship, and if so, how does that make a difference in your ministry?

Appendix A: Guides for Interview, Focus Group, and Survey

13. Are there things you can't do in person that you can do on DCM for your ministry or discipleship, and if so, how does that make a difference in your ministry?
14. What value do you see for using DCM in ministry for young adults?
15. What type of support do you need more of in order to utilize DCM for your young adult ministry?

FOCUS GROUP

1. How have you been able to maintain your relationships with Adventist friends?
2. What are the most important factors to build close rapport with Adventist friends?
3. How has DCM related to maintaining and deepening relationships with Adventist workers?
4. How have you been able to start spiritual conversation with Adventist friends?
5. What type of spiritual topics are you interested in?
6. Has DCM influenced your conversion process or spiritual growth, and if so, how has it related to the process?
7. Has DCM affected your thoughts and cultures?
8. Personally, what do you think the positives and negatives are of DCM in spiritual growth?
9. Are there things you can't do on DCM that you can do in person for spiritual life, and if so, how does that make a difference in growth?
10. Are there things you can't do in person that you can do on DCM for spiritual life, and if so, how does that make a difference in your growth?
11. What would you say about using DCM for spiritual life?

SURVEY

1. Please select your choice below.
    - You have read the provided information about this survey.
    - You voluntarily agree to participate.

Appendix A: Guides for Interview, Focus Group, and Survey

- You are 18 years of age or older.
    a. Agree
    b. Disagree
2. What is your primary initiative in your field?
    a. Waldensian student
    b. Global mission pioneer
    c. Bible worker
    d. Center of influence
    e. Pastor
    f. Other

    **Please specify if you have other roles than those listed above.

    _____

3. How old are you?
    a. 20–25
    b. 26–30
    c. 31–40
    d. 41–50
    e. 51–60
    f. 61–70
    g. More than 70 years
4. What is your gender?
    a. Female
    b. Male
5. How long have you worked in your field?
    a. Under 2 years
    b. 2–5 years
    c. 5–10 years
    d. 10–20 years
    e. More than 20 years

Appendix A: Guides for Interview, Focus Group, and Survey

6. How many non-Christian young adult friends (age 20–38) do you have?

    a. 1–2

    b. 3–4

    c. 5–6

    d. 6–10

    e. More than 10

7. How have you usually been able to create the first connections with young adults? Select all applicable:

    a. Friend connection

    b. Online

    c. Spontaneous encounter (mall, market, street, classroom)

    d. Institutionally organized activities (cultural center)

    e. Other (please specify)

8. How have you maintained your relationships with the young adults?

    a. Spontaneous hanging out (meal, sports, tea)

    b. Institutionally organized activities (cooking, language class, health, etc.)

    c. Work or learning related activities (school projects, language exchange)

    d. Other (please specify)

9. What are the most important factors to establish close relationships with young adult friends in your interaction? *Please select a maximum of two.*

    a. Caring (e.g., willing to help, expression of affection, being available)

    b. Being open and genuine

    c. Exemplary life (e.g., lifestyle, spirituality, ethics)

    d. Other (please specify)

10. What opportunities allow you to introduce spiritual topics to your young adult friends? *Please select a maximum of two.*

Appendix A: Guides for Interview, Focus Group, and Survey

   a. Religious questions from friends (e.g., Christianity, Adventist)
   b. Life questions and issues from friends
   c. Offering testimonies
   d. Other (please specify)

11. What types of spiritual topics have you used to engage with young adults? *Please select a maximum of three.*
    a. Salvation
    b. Prayer
    c. Character of God
    d. Human suffering
    e. The authenticity of the Bible
    f. Religious rituals
    g. World religion
    h. Sabbath
    i. Creation
    j. Dreams and visions
    k. End-time events
    l. Purpose of life
    m. Prophets
    n. Other (please specify)

12. What are the most critical factors to deepen your spiritual interaction with young adult friends? Please select all applicable.
    a. Curiosity
    b. Previously established trust and spiritual talks
    c. Initiative from young adult friends
    d. Initiative from Adventist workers
    e. Other (please specify)

13. What type of DCM do you use when you interact with young adult friends? *Please select the three platforms you use the most.*
    a. Facebook

Appendix A: Guides for Interview, Focus Group, and Survey

   b. Twitter
   c. YouTube
   d. Instagram
   e. Snapchat
   f. WhatsApp
   g. Telegram
   h. Signal
   i. Email
   j. Zoom
   k. Google meet
   l. TikTok
   m. Other (please specify)

14. How much of your interaction with young adults has been done on digital communication media in the past twelve months?
    a. 0%
    b. 1–25%
    c. 26–50%
    d. 51–75%
    e. 76–100%

15. During the past twelve months, how many times, if any, have you been able to interact with your young adult friends in person?
    a. Every day
    b. A few times a week
    c. About once a week
    d. A few times a month
    e. Once a month
    f. Less than once a month
    g. Never

16. What are the main values of using DCM for young adult ministries in your mission field? *Please select a maximum of four.*

Appendix A: Guides for Interview, Focus Group, and Survey

   a. Maintaining and strengthening relationships with young adult friends (e.g., keeping in touch regardless of barriers of time and space)
   b. Spiritual interactions with young adult friends
   c. Providing security and confidentiality
   d. Compensating for language barriers
   e. Connecting with friends and families in your home country
   f. Communicating with leaders and coworkers (report, discussion, etc.)
   g. Organizing events
   h. Other (please specify)

17. During the past twelve months, how many times, if any, have you been able to interact with your young adult friends in person for spiritual topics?
    a. Every day
    b. A few times a week
    c. About once a week
    d. A few times a month
    e. Once a month
    f. Less than once a month
    g. Never

18. During the past twelve months, how many times, if any, have you been able to interact with your young adult friends via DCM for spiritual topics?
    a. Every day
    b. A few times a week
    c. About once a week
    d. A few times a month
    e. Once a month
    f. Less than once a month
    g. Never

Appendix A: Guides for Interview, Focus Group, and Survey

19. During the past twelve months, how many times, if any, have you been able to interact with your young adult friends in person for spiritual topics?

    a. Every day

    b. A few times a week

    c. About once a week

    d. A few times a month

    e. Once a month

    f. Less than once a month

    g. Never

20. Is the time you spend on DCM for personal or ministry/work?

    a. Personal

    b. Ministry/work

    c. Mixture of both (please specify [e.g., 30:70])

21. How much has DCM been useful for maintaining and developing relationships with your young adult friends?

    a. Extremely effective

    b. Very effective

    c. Moderately effective

    d. Slightly effective

    e. Not effective at all

22. What are your primary communication modes in interaction with young adults on DCM? Please select a maximum of three.

    a. Text chat

    b. Voice chat

    c. Video chat

    d. Voice message

    e. Social media posts and comments

    f. Other

Appendix A: Guides for Interview, Focus Group, and Survey

23. What is your usual form of communication with young adult friends on DCM?
    a. Group
    b. One-on-one
    c. A mixture of both (please specify [e.g., 50:50])
24. Has the COVID-19 situation significantly increased your digital communication with young adult friends?
    a. Extremely likely
    b. Moderately likely
    c. Slightly likely
    d. Neither likely nor unlikely
    e. Slightly unlikely
    f. Moderately unlikely
25. What are your primary communication languages when you interact with young adult friends on DCM?
    a. English
    b. Local
    c. A mixture of both. (Please specify the ratio between group and one-on-one [e.g., 30:70 or 50:50].)
26. What type of media formats have been the most effective for you to create spiritual engagement with young adults on DCM? *Please select a maximum of three.*
    a. Video materials (video file, YouTube link)
    b. Image materials (memes, graphics, pictures)
    c. Audio materials (audio files, podcast)
    d. Text materials (e-book, e-brochure)
    e. Conversations (verbal, text)
    f. Other (please specify)
27. How important is DCM to your young adult ministry in overall?
    a. Extremely important
    b. Very important

Appendix A: Guides for Interview, Focus Group, and Survey

    c. Moderately important

    d. Slightly important

    e. Not at all important

28. How has DCM negatively affected your life in field? *Please select all if applicable.*

    a. Misunderstandings

    b. Time consumption

    c. Shallow conversation and relationship

    d. Security concerns

    e. Pressure to respond all the time

    f. Other (please specify)

29. What are the non-replaceable roles of in-person (face to face) communication? (e.g., what DCM cannot replace). *Please select a maximum of two.*

    a. Human touch and feeling

    b. Providing security

    c. Compensate language barriers

    d. Focused interaction without distraction

    e. Other (please specify)

30. What support do you need more of in order to utilize DCM for young adult ministry? *Select a maximum of two.*

    a. Language skills

    b. Platform knowledge

    c. Cultural knowledge about young adults

    d. Sharable materials

    e. Finance

    f. Other (please specify)

Appendix B

Semi-structured Interview and Focus Group Participants Reference Sheet

Method/Date	Gender	Code
Interview 07/01/20	Male	AW-1
Interview 07/02/20	Female	AW-2
Interview 07/02/20	Male	AW-3
Interview 07/03/20	Male	AW-4
Interview 06/30/20	Female	AW-5
Interview 06/28/20	Male	AW-6
Interview 06/28/20	Female	AW-7
Interview 06/29/20	Female	AW-8
Interview 06/29/20	Male	AW-9
Interview 07/05/20	Female	AW-10
Interview 07/13/20	Male	AW-11

Appendix B: Semi-structured Interview and Focus Group Participants

Method/Date	Gender	Code
Interview 06/26/20	Male	AW-12
Interview 06/26/20	Female	AW-13
Interview 07/02/20	Male	AW-14
Interview 07/06/20	Male	AW-15
Interview 07/01/20	Female	AW-16
Interview 07/14/20	Female	AW-17
Interview 07/13/20	Female	AW-18
Interview 07/06/20	Male	AW-19
Interview 07/06/20	Male	AW-20
Interview 06/30/20	Male	AW-21
Interview 07/05/20	Male	AW-23
Interview 07/07/20	Male	AW-25
Interview 07/02/20	Male	AW-27
Interview 06/29/20	Female	AW-28
Interview 06/29/20	Female	AW-29
Interview 07/07/20	Female	AW-30
Interview 07/07/20	Male	AW-31

Appendix B: Semi-structured Interview and Focus Group Participants

Method/Date	Gender	Code
Interview 06/26/20	Female	AW-32
Interview 07/08/20	Male	AW-33
Interview 07/03/20	Female	AW-34
Interview 07/03/20	Male	AW-36
Interview 06/28/20	Female	AW-37
Interview 06/28/20	Male	AW-38
Interview 07/08/20	Male	AW-39
Interview 07/05/20	Male	AW-40
Interview 07/08/20	Female	AW-41
Interview 07/01/20	Male	AW-43
Interview 06/30/20	Male	AW-44
Interview 06/30/20	Male	AW-45
Focus Group 09/13/20	Female	MBB-46
Focus Group 09/13/20	Female	MBB-48
Focus Group 09/13/20	Male	MBB-49
Focus Group 09/13/20	Male	MBB-50
Focus Group 09/13/20	Male	MBB-51

Appendix C

Survey Result Report

Q8: How have you usually been able to create the first connection with young adult friends? Select all if applicable.

#	Answer	%	Count
1	Friend connection	36.67%	33
2	Online	5.56%	5
3	Spontaneous encounter (e.g., market, school, social club)	41.11%	37
4	Institutionally organized activities (e.g., COI, health expo, conferences)	11.11%	10
5	Other (please specify)	5.56%	5
	Total	100%	90

Q9: How have you maintained your relationships with young adults?

Appendix C: Survey Result Report

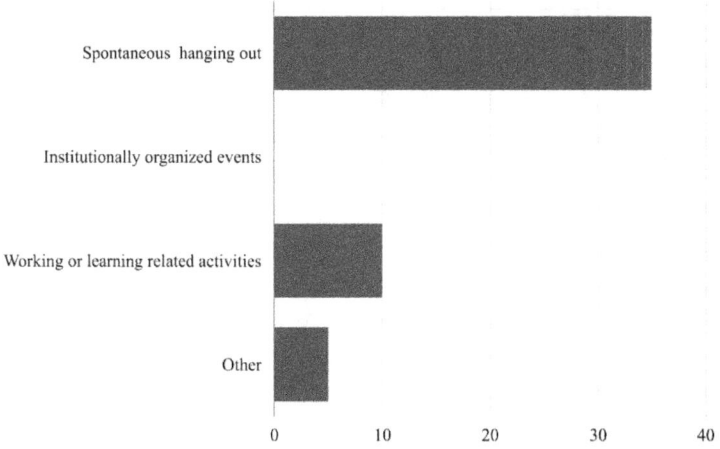

Q11: What are the most important factors to establish close relationships with young adult friends in your interaction? *Please select a maximum of two.*

#	Answer	%	Count
4	Respect	4.44%	4
7	Other	1.11%	1
3	Exemplary life (e.g., lifestyle, spirituality, ethics)	18.89%	17
1	Caring (e.g., willing to help, expression of affection, being available)	45.56%	41
2	Being open and genuine	30%	27
	Total	100%	90

Q13: What types of spiritual topics have you used to engage with young adults? Please select a maximum of three.

#	Answer	%	Count
1	Human suffering	7.56%	9
2	Prayer	18.49%	22

Appendix C: Survey Result Report

#	Answer	%	Count
3	Salvation	4.20%	5
5	Jesus	7.56%	9
7	The authenticity of the Bible	5.88%	7
8	Other (please specify)	0.84%	1
11	Character of God	14.29%	17
12	Religious ritual	2.52%	3
13	World religion	5.88%	7
14	Sabbath	9.24%	11
15	Creation	2.52%	3
16	Dreams and visions	1.68%	2
17	End-time events	5.04%	6
18	Purpose of life	8.40%	10
19	Prophets	5.88%	7
	Total	100%	119

Q14: During the past twelve months, how many times, if any, have you been able to interact with your young adult friends in person for spiritual topics ?

#	Answer	%	Count
1	Every day	2.04%	1
2	A few times a week	28.57%	14
3	About once a week	22.45%	11
4	A few times a month	18.37%	9
5	Once a month	6.12%	3
6	Less than once a month	20.41%	10
7	Never	2.04%	1
	Total	100%	49

Appendix C: Survey Result Report

Q19: During the past twelve months, how many times, if any, have you been able to interact with your young adult friends in person?

#	Answer	%	Count
1	Every day	4.08%	2
2	A few times a week	38.78%	19
3	About once a week	22.45%	11
4	A few times a month	18.37%	9
5	Once a month	10.20%	5
6	Less than once a month	4.08%	2
7	Never	2.04%	1
	Total	100%	49

Q21: What are the main values of using digital communication media (DCM) for young adult ministries in your mission field? Please select a maximum of four.

#	Answer	%	Count
7	Maintaining and strengthening relationships with young adult friends (e.g., keeping in touch regardless of barriers of time and space)	28.57%	42
6	Spiritual interactions with young adult friends	16.33%	24
3	Connecting with friends and families in your home country	14.97%	22
4	Communicating with leaders and coworkers (report, discussion, etc.)	13.61%	20
5	Organizing events	9.52%	14
1	Compensate language barriers	8.16%	12
2	Providing security and confidentiality	8.16%	12
8	Other (please specify)	0.68%	1
	Total	100%	147

Appendix C: Survey Result Report

Q23: Is the time you spend on DCM for personal or ministry/work . . .

#	Answer	%	Count
1	Personal	12.24%	6
2	Ministry/work	12.24%	6
3	A mixture of both (Please specify the ratio between personal and ministry, e.g., 30:70 or 50:50.)	75.51%	37
	Total	100%	49

A mixture of both (Please specify the ratio between personal and ministry, e.g., 30:70 or 50:50.)

50:50	hard to measure, sorry
40:60	50:50
60:40	50:50
60:40	60:40
50:50	40:60
60:40	50:50
50:50	40:60
60:40	60:40
60/40	60:40
70:30	40:60
70:30	50:50
60:40	70:30
70:30	60:40
80/20	60:40

Appendix C: Survey Result Report

A mixture of both (Please specify the ratio between personal and ministry, e.g., 30:70 or 50:50.)

30:70
50:50
50:50
50:50
50:50
30:70
60:40

Q24: How much of your interaction with young adults was done on DCM in the past twelve months?

#	Answer	%	Count
1	76–100%	20.41%	10
2	51–75%	22.45%	11
3	26–50%	38.78%	19
4	1–25%	18.37%	9
5	0%	0.00%	0
	Total	100%	49

Q25: What type of DCM do you use when you interact with young adult friends? *Please select the three platforms you use the most.*

#	Answer	%	Count
1	Facebook	14.52%	18
2	Twitter	0.00%	0
3	YouTube	4.03%	5

Appendix C: Survey Result Report

#	Answer	%	Count
4	Instagram	25.00%	31
5	Snapchat	0.00%	0
6	WhatsApp	35.48%	44
7	Telegram	4.84%	6
8	Signal	0.00%	0
9	Email	0.00%	0
10	Zoom	13.71%	17
11	Google meet	0.00%	0
12	Other (Please specify other platforms if you have any)	2.42%	3
13	TikTok	0.00%	0
	Total	100%	124

Q27: During the past twelve months, how many times, if any, have you been able to interact with your young adult friends via DCM for spiritual topics?

#	Answer	%	Count
1	Every day	2.04%	1
2	A few times a week	20.41%	10
3	About once a week	20.41%	10
4	A few times a month	32.65%	16
5	Once a month	4.08%	2
6	Less than once a month	18.37%	9
7	Never	2.04%	1
	Total	100%	49

Q28: How much has DCM been useful for maintaining and developing relationships with your young adult friends?

Appendix C: Survey Result Report

#	Answer	%	Count
12	Extremely effective	20.41%	10
13	Very effective	48.98%	24
14	Moderately effective	26.53%	13
15	Slightly effective	4.08%	2
16	Not effective at all	0.00%	0
	Total	100%	49

Q35: What are your primary communication modes for young adults on DCM? *Please select a maximum of three.*

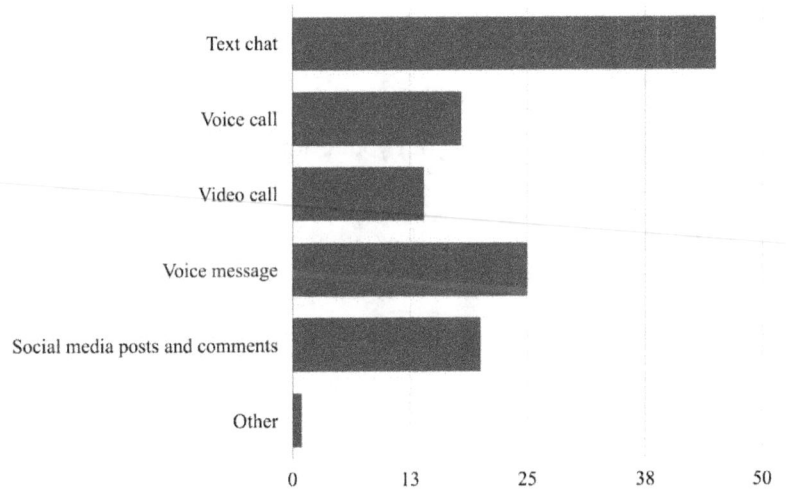

Q36: What types of media format have been effective for you to create spiritual engagement with young adults on DCM? *Please select a maximum of three.*

Appendix C: Survey Result Report

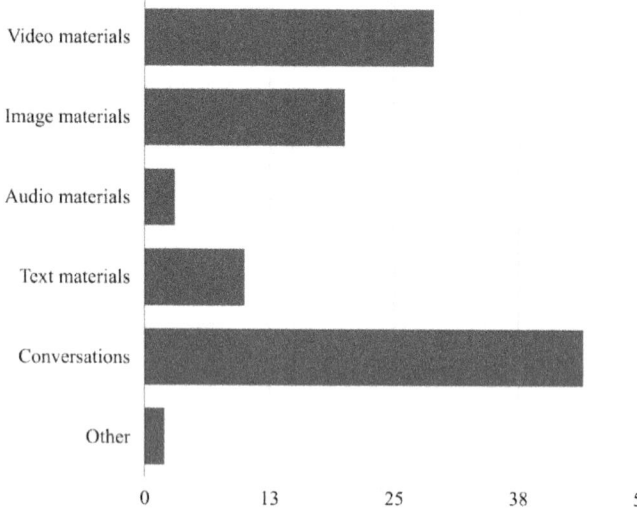

Q38: How important is DCM to your young adult ministry overall?

#	Answer	%	Count
1	Extremely important	26.53%	13
2	Very important	38.78%	19
3	Moderately important	32.65%	16
4	Slightly important	2.04%	1
5	Not at all important	0.00%	0
	Total	100%	49

Q40: How has DCM negatively affected your life in field? *Please select all if applicable.*

#	Answer	%	Count
1	Shallow conversation and relationships	13.76%	15

Appendix C: Survey Result Report

#	Answer	%	Count
2	Time consumption	24.77%	27
4	Misunderstandings	9.17%	10
5	Security concerns	25.69%	28
6	Other (please specify)	3.67%	4
7	Pressure to respond all the time	22.94%	25
	Total	100%	109

Q42: What support do you need more of in order to utilize DCM for young adult ministry? *Select a maximum of two.*

#	Answer	%	Count
2	Sharable materials	35.29%	30
3	Language skills	38.82%	33
4	Finance	0.00%	0
5	Other (please specify)	1.18%	1
6	Platform knowledge	7.06%	6
7	Cultural knowledge about young adults	17.65%	15
	Total	100%	85

Q45: What opportunities allow you to introduce spiritual topics to your young adult friends? *Please select a maximum of two.*

#	Answer	%	Count
1	Religious questions from friends (e.g., Christianity, Adventist)	47.67%	41
2	Life questions and issues from friends	43.02%	37
3	Other	1.16%	1
4	Offering testimonies	8.14%	7
	Total	100%	86

Appendix C: Survey Result Report

Q46: What are the most critical factors to deepen your spiritual interaction with young adult friends? *Please select all if applicable.*

#	Answer	%	Count
1	Curiosity	27.62%	29
2	Previously established trust and spiritual talks	42.86%	45
3	Initiative from young adult friends	20.00%	21
4	Other (please specify)	4.76%	5
5	Initiative from Adventist workers	4.76%	5
	Total	100%	105

Q47: How much has DCM been effective for spiritual interaction between you and your young adult friends?

#	Answer	%	Count
12	Extremely effective	6.12%	3
13	Very effective	26.53%	13
14	Moderately effective	44.90%	22
15	Slightly effective	20.41%	10
16	Not effective at all	2.04%	1
	Total	100%	49

Q31: What is your usual form of communication with young adult friends on DCM?

#	Answer	%	Count
1	Group	0.00%	0
2	One-on-one	67.35%	33
3	A mixture of both (Please specify the ratio between group and one-on-one, e.g., 30:70 or 50:50.)	32.65%	16
	Total	100%	49

Appendix C: Survey Result Report

A mixture of both (Please specify the ratio between group and one-on-one, e.g., 30:70 or 50:50.)

95% personal, 5% group	30:70
25:75	25:75
60:40	20:80
70:30	20:80
30:70	70:30
30:70	30:70
40:60	30:70
30:70	

Q54: Has the COVID-19 situation significantly increased your digital communication with young adult friends?

#	Answer	%	Count
18	Extremely likely	34.69%	17
19	Moderately likely	40.82%	20
20	Slightly likely	22.45%	11
21	Neither likely nor unlikely	0.00%	0
22	Slightly unlikely	0.00%	0
23	Moderately unlikely	0.00%	0
24	Extremely unlikely	2.04%	1
	Total	100%	49

Q50: What are your primary communication languages when you interact with young adult friends on DCM?

#	Answer	%	Count
1	English	42.86%	21
2	Local language	55.10%	27

Appendix C: Survey Result Report

#	Answer	%	Count
3	Your native language (non-English)	2.04%	1
	Total	100%	49

Q49: What are the non-replaceable roles of in-person (face-to-face) communication, e.g., what DCM cannot replace)? Please select a maximum of two.

#	Answer	%	Count
1	Human touch and feeling	47.73%	42
2	Providing security	7.95%	7
3	Compensate language barriers	12.50%	11
4	Focused interaction without distraction	27.27%	24
5	Other (please specify)	4.55%	4
	Total	100%	88

Appendix D

Lecture Notes on Findings for Brainstorming Group

1. Toward Being Together with Young Adults in the Digital Middle East and North Africa

2. New Technologies and Worldviews (Hiebert 2009)

    "New technologies, such as cars and the Internet, emerge, and these transform the underlying worldviews" (Hiebert 2009, 32).

3. Ingredients for New Culture (Castells 2000)

    - The information technology revolution
    - The economic crisis
    - The flourishing of cultural social movements (libertarianism, human rights, feminism)

4. Cultural Goods and Worldview (Crouch 2008)

    "The danger of reducing culture to worldview is that we may miss the most distinctive thing about culture, which is that cultural goods have a life of their own. They reshape the world in unpredictable ways" (Crouch 2008, 69).

5. Technology and Mission

    "Our mission is significantly changed because today in much of the world, digital technology is not optional. It has fundamentally altered the way we live.... Therefore we need to find authentic ways of living the Christian life and witnessing within the digital age" (Kim 2019).

Appendix D: Lecture Notes on Findings for Brainstorming Group

6. Influence of Technology (Lewis Mumford [1895–1990])

    "The clock, not steam-engine, is the key machine of the modern industrial age" (Mumford 1934).

7. RQ1: What are Adventist frontline workers' young adult ministry practices for relationship building and spiritual interaction?

8. RQ2: How is digital communication media (DCM) impacting Adventist workers' young adult ministry practices?

9. RQ3: What are the non-replaceable roles of in-person communication in Adventist workers' young adult ministry practices?

10. RQ4: What roles has DCM played in the relationship building and the spiritual interaction of young adult Adventist Muslim-background believers?

11. Relationship-building process

12. Findings: Relationship building

    - DCM did not play a critical role in the first connection.
    - Adventist workers obtain opportunities to connect with MENA young adults through places and activities in which young people are often involved.
    - Adventist workers encountered young adults most frequently through different affinity connections: language schools, universities, sports, introductions by friends, social clubs, and day-to-day activities.
    - "Almost 100 percent of my non-Christian friends I met at the university" (AW-25).
    - "A friend of mine introduced me to his friend, and then the new friend connected me to another friend. In this way, my relationship circle with young adults is getting bigger every year" (AW-38).

13. Findings: Relationship building

    - MENA young adults are open to relationships with non-Muslim outsiders if they share common interests such as sports, health, languages, cultures, school activities, and hobbies.
    - A young non-Christian passed by the building. Drawn by the guitar playing, he walked into the church and sat down to listen.

Appendix D: Lecture Notes on Findings for Brainstorming Group

According to the worker, "He asked me, 'Oh, you play the guitar?' Then we became friends" (AW-31).

14. Findings: Relationship building
    - The relationships between Adventist workers and young adults are maintained by social interactions and are deepened by trust.
    - "In the Middle East, eating together is very essential to relationship" (AW-1).
    - Social activities are initiated by mutual desire for connection.
    - "We tried to meet as many as often as possible, like hanging out in a café, or having a sport activity" (MBB-50).

15. Findings: Relationship building
    - When Adventist workers demonstrate care, openness, and exemplary lives, this helps to establish deep trust.
    - Young adults experience care when their innermost feelings and frustration are heard and acknowledged.
    - "When you are real, when you show the real you with your weaknesses and good things, the person trusts you because they feel that you don't hide like others" (AW-37).
    - "They see that you always speak good words without bad words and gossiping, respecting the others. So they see that you are different" (AW-4).

16. Findings: Impact of DCM on relationship building
    - DCM plays a significant role in maintaining and strengthening relationships among Adventist workers and young adults.
    - DCM provides them with opportunities to learn about each other.
    - "They ask my Instagram and Facebook ID even before my mobile number" (AW-18).
    - For MENA young adults, asking for someone's DCM information at a first-time meeting is considered socially acceptable.
    - "We can understand what they like to do, what they like to talk about, or how they like to express their feelings and thoughts. So this is the way it helps us to get closer and establish a stronger relationship" (AW-23).

Appendix D: Lecture Notes on Findings for Brainstorming Group

- "I felt the need of seeing my friends and spending time together. Nevertheless, the fact is that [DCM] helped us a lot to build bridges that I think physically would have been longer" (AW-43).

17. Findings: Impact of DCM on relationship building
    - DCM enables Adventist workers to approach young adults with relevant topics.
    - "Once, someone posted a picture of a crying woman on WhatsApp. I was able to have conversations about the status. I used it to start a new conversation" (AW-45).
    - Adventist workers experienced young adults as more open and expressive online than in real life.
    - "Most of my friends behave more conservative and traditional in person than on DCM. When they use DCM, they open themselves in a way that they would never do in person" (AW-25).
    - "We can save time [through DCM]. It is important because it creates the links, it gives the trust, and it gives time to build the friendship" (MBB-50).

18. Findings: Impact of DCM on relationship building
    - MENA young adults experience care when Adventist workers utilize DCM to regularly check in on their young adult connections, overcoming the barriers of time and space.
    - "We cannot maintain relationships if we don't send messages. When I send them a message, we keep our relationship" (AW-20).
    - "You have an opportunity to enter that person's life that God can use, at any moment of the day. So it is just an amazing opportunity to have that instant connection. It's invaluable. The ministry of presence at any time is a huge blessing" (AW-2).

19. Findings: Impact of DCM on relationship building
    - The importance of DCM for young adult ministry has increased during the COVID-19 pandemic.
    - "[DCM] has shortened the distance, firstly. It has allowed us to be connected in this lockdown. I couldn't meet with my friends in person during the past four months" (AW-44).

Appendix D: Lecture Notes on Findings for Brainstorming Group

20. Findings: Spiritual interactions
    - Adventist workers initiated spiritual interaction with young adults most frequently through religious questions and life issues.
    - MENA young adults have little to no aversion to asking and receiving religious questions.
    - "In my experience, 90 percent of my non-Christian friends usually ask me about my religion and related topics from the first day" (AW-18).
    - Life issues created opportunities for them to interact with young adults about spiritual topics.
    - "I think life issues could ignite the spiritual conversation" (MBB-51).
    - Young adults become willing to share their innermost life issues when trust is built through Adventist workers' care, openness, and exemplary lives.

21. Findings: Spiritual interactions
    - Spiritual interactions among Adventist workers and young adults are deepened and moved forward through establishing trust-based relationships and engaging the natural curiosity of MENA young adults.
    - "If I already have some trust built, we get to the point. They understand that I have some spiritual interests, and they are comfortable" (AW-41).
    - "I was so curious, and I had a lot of questions. I asked my Adventist friends a lot of questions, and I kept seeking answers" (MBB-48).
    - The most engaging spiritual topics are prayer and God's character, because those two subjects are what young adults desire answers to when they deal with unsolved life questions.

22. Findings: Impact of DCM on spiritual interactions
    - DCM enables Adventist workers to hold spiritual conversations with young adult friends.
    - "I do Bible studies through WhatsApp conversation instead of sitting down and opening a Bible. That is how I'm sharing the word of God" (AW-16).

Appendix D: Lecture Notes on Findings for Brainstorming Group

- "Sometimes I send Bible verses by WhatsApp and ask them to read. To make sure that they read it, I ask them to send me the reflection on what they read and what they understood from the verses" (AW-15).
- "The biggest value is that you can get more [spiritual] knowledge. When you have a question, you can quickly send it to one of the leaders or someone who knows the Bible better so that he can explain to you. Yeah, this is the important thing" (MBB-49).

23. Findings: Impact of DCM on spiritual interactions
    - DCM provides them with safe platforms that allow them to avoid direct conflicts and security issues when they share spiritual messages with young adults.
    - "We would have like some kind of difficult questions that can be answered, for example: "Is Jesus God?" Or talking about their own religion. I could share videos that can answer such questions on WhatsApp. I would not be comfortable to answer that questions directly as a friend because maybe it can create problems between us. Maybe it's a very hard topic that can destroy our relationship if I would talk with them in person. But I can share a video with them on DCM" (AW-6).
    - "I would say that [DCM] . . . makes people feel safer about learning this new information about praying, and I think it is safer for them because it's more like I'm here, but I'm not here. It helped a lot for us to break through cultural barriers that you wouldn't easily break in person, that the social pressure wouldn't let you in, but technology can make you invisible" (AW-43).

24. Findings: Impact of DCM on spiritual interactions
    - DCM provides them with safe platforms that allow them to avoid direct conflicts and security issues when they share spiritual messages with young adults.
    - "I can guarantee that they will have the freedom of questioning and doubting [on DCM]. And that's what's most important, because usually when we are confronted by the society, we are afraid to change because we are going to be judged by our family. We can be threatened. We can be, I mean, [critiqued by] society. But social

Appendix D: Lecture Notes on Findings for Brainstorming Group

media, what it gives, it gives confidence and freedom to doubt. And this doubting will push them to ask more questions" (MBB-50).

25. Findings: Limitations of DCM for young adult practices
    - DCM frequently leads to distraction and addiction, becoming time-consuming.
    - "You are so into the network and the internet, browsing and browsing and
    - browsing. Finally, you find that you are lost somewhere. You don't even realize how much time you spent" (AW-32).
    - "[DCM] is a big distraction in many ways. There's so much to take your time and to take your energy, you know, Facebook and all these things. Many times, we're so busy checking our phones we miss out on other opportunities that we could have connected with people" (AW-5).
    - Some Adventist workers experience shallow conversations and relationships with young adults on DCM.

26. Findings: Limitations of DCM for young adult ministry practices
    - Some Adventist workers experience shallow conversations and relationships with young adults on DCM.
    - Young adults communicate without real communication on DCM. That's a challenge.
    - "You are part of a WhatsApp group. They see our messages and then occasionally, they'll send a brief yes or no, or okay. You may feel that communication has happened, but really it hasn't. Just because you're informed doesn't mean that we've communicated. It is very normal to have these kinds of interactions [on DCM]" (AW-9).
    - Lack of human touch: physical behaviors and focused interaction.
    - In-person communication allows for emotional bonding through physical behaviors that cannot be replaced by digital communication.
    - In-person communication also allows Adventist workers to focus on interactions with young adults without distractions.

Appendix D: Lecture Notes on Findings for Brainstorming Group

27. Findings: Limitations of DCM for young adult ministry practices
    - "It's not that you can't see them. You can, if you have a video call. You can see them. But, yeah, there are some limitations, like touch[ing], putting a hand on their shoulder, and hugging" (AW-45).
    - In-person communication also allows Adventist workers to focus on interactions with young adults without distractions
    - "When I'm in in-person meetings, I dedicate 100 percent of my time to them. I don't pay attention to social media—to any distractions or to the phone or anything else. I'm just with them, and I give my full attention" (AW-14).
    - In-person communication and DCM are supplementary in Adventist workers' young adult ministries.

28. Observations
    - Expectation: Frontline workers of the Middle East and North Africa Union Mission of the Seventh-day Adventist Church can utilize digital communication more effectively for their young adult ministries.
    - Disappointment: Several Adventist workers stated their firm conviction that mission must be face-to-face and interpersonal. Many interviewees had not considered the connection between DCM and their in-field ministries. In fact, for young adult ministry, they considered DCM a nonessential tool or a method inferior to in-person communication.

29. Conclusion
    - DCM catalyzed interactions after an initial spontaneous in-person encounter; created a sense of care and togetherness, which helped Adventist workers establish trust; and provided platforms and security for spiritual interaction.
    - I also observe the limitations of DCM, which include that it is highly time-consuming, contributes to shallow interactions, and lacks the element of human touch. DCM is embedded into Adventist workers' young adult ministries, whether or not the workers recognized the impact.

Appendix D: Lecture Notes on Findings for Brainstorming Group

30. Gaps
    - Institutional strategies but no model practices for workers. The focus is on security issues and technology.

Appendix E

Best DCM Practices for Young Adults

PARTICIPANTS:

*Please share tips and ideas based on the lecture that other workers can utilize daily or should keep in their minds while they engage with non-Christian young adult friends.

*Digital communication media: Email, WhatsApp, Facebook, Instagram, Zoom, etc.

*Young Adults: Non-Christian friends between the ages of twenty and thirty-eight

For Building Relationship after the First Encounter

*Keywords: Catalyzing interactions, mingling, learning about each other, relevant talking points, open expression

1.
2.

For Deepening Relationship

*Keywords: Creating a sense of togetherness and care, increasing trust, overcoming barriers of time and space

1.
2.

Appendix E: Best DCM Practices for Young Adults

For Spiritual Interactions

*Keywords: Promoting spiritual interactions, small group, Bible study, discussion, security

1.
2.

For Avoiding Limitations of Digital Communication Media

*Keywords: Time-consuming, misunderstanding, interrupted interaction, lack of physical behaviors (hugging, facial)

1.
2.

Additional Tips and Ideas for Utilizing DCM to Minister to Young Adults

1.
2.

Vita

ChanMin Chung was born December 16, 1977, to Jungyeo Kim and Bongchae Chung. He grew up in Seoul, the capital city of South Korea, and Wonju-si, the most populous city in Gangwon province of the country. In 2000, he earned a bachelor of arts in theology at the Shamyook University in Seoul.

In 2002, ChanMin joined the Adventist Media Center at the Korean Union Conference of Seventh-day Adventists in Seoul as a program director, with a focus on video production for various church ministries. In 2005, ChanMin married SuKyoung, who was a member of the Golden Angels, a singing Adventist missionary group. In 2010, together, they moved to Lebanon as intercultural workers. ChanMin became the production manager at Hope Channel Arabic (Alwaad TV). In 2014, he was elected as the communication director of the Middle East and North Africa Union Mission of Seventh-day Adventists. In July 2018, the mission asked him to lead the media center, the social media outreach initiative, and the communication department. On April 21, 2021, the mission formed Trans-Media Group MENA to coordinate all forms of media for the church's mission, including television, radio, web, digital evangelism, follow-up, translation services, books, publications, tracts, and church-based resources, as well as organizational communication. ChanMin was appointed as the managing director of the media group and as the field secretary of the mission. In 2022, ChanMin and his family relocated to Maryland in the United States, where the church's headquarters are located. Chanmin serves as the vice president for global media and engagement for Hope Channel International at the General Conference of Seventh-day Adventists.

Vita

ChanMin completed his master of arts in Islamic studies from Middle East University in 2018 and will graduate with a doctor of global leadership from Fuller Theological Seminary in 2022. ChanMin and SuKyoung have two children.

In 2022, ChanMin and his family relocated to Maryland in the United States, where the church's headquarters are located. ChanMin served as the senior director of television distribution for Hope Channel International at the General Conference of Seventh-day Adventists and was appointed as the Vice President for Global Media and Engagement in 2024.

Bibliography

Abdulla, Rasha. "Egypt's Media in the Midst of Revolution." *Carnegie Endowment for International Peace*, July 16, 2014. https://carnegieendowment.org/research/2014/07/egypts-media-in-the-midst-of-revolution?lang=en.

Alahmed, Anas. "Voice of the Arabs Radio: Its Effects and Political Power During the Nasser Era (1953–1967)." *SSRN Electronic Journal* (2011).

Allagui, Ilhem. "The Changing Nature of Socialization Among Arab Youth: Insights from Online Practice." In *Digital Middle East: State and Society in the Information Age*, edited by Mohamed Zayani, 33–59. New York: Oxford University Press, 2018. Kindle.

Auxier, Brooke, et al. "Parenting Children in the Age of Screens." *Pew Research Center*, July 28, 2020. https://www.pewresearch.org/internet/2020/07/28/parenting-children-in-the-age-of-screens/.

Bachmann, Reinhard, and Akbar Zaheer, eds. *Handbook of Trust Research*. Cheltenham, UK: Elgar, 2008.

Bernard, Harvey Russell. *Research Methods in Anthropology: Qualitative and Quantitative Approaches*. 4th ed. Lanham, MD: AltaMira, 2006.

Bhattacharya, Rajeev, et al. "A Formal Model of Trust Based on Outcomes." *Academy of Management Review* 23 (1998) 459–72. https://doi.org/10.5465/amr.1998.926621.

Bolger, Ryan K., and Kutter Callaway, eds. *Techno-Sapiens in a Networked Era: Becoming Digital Neighbors*. Eugene, OR: Cascade, 2020.

boyd, danah. "Friendship." In *Hanging Out, Messing Around, and Geeking Out: Kids Living and Learning with New Media*, edited by Mizuko Itō, 79–115. Cambridge: MIT Press, 2010.

Bunker, Barbara Benedict, and Jeffrey Z. Rubin, eds. *Conflict, Cooperation, and Justice: Essays Inspired by the Work of Morton Deutsch*. San Francisco: Jossey-Bass, 1995.

Campbell, Heidi A., and Stephen Garner. *Networked Theology: Negotiating Faith in Digital Culture*. Grand Rapids: Baker Academic, 2016. Kindle.

Castells, Manuel. *The Internet Galaxy: Reflections on the Internet, Business, and Society*. Oxford: Oxford University Press, 2002.

———. *Networks of Outrage and Hope: Social Movements in the Internet Age*. Cambridge: Polity, 2015. Kindle.

———. *The Rise of the Network Society*. Oxford: Blackwell, 2000.

Castells, Manuel, et al. *Mobile Communication and Society: A Global Perspective*. Cambridge: MIT Press, 2007.

Bibliography

Clark-Gordon, Cathlin V., et al. "Anonymity and Online Self-Disclosure: A Meta-Analysis." *Communication Reports* 32 (2019) 98–111. https://doi.org/10.1080/08934215.2019.1607516.

Cloete, Anita L. "Living in a Digital Culture: The Need for Theological Reflection." *Hervormde Teologiese Studies; Pretoria* 71 (2015) 1–7.

Creswell, John W. *Qualitative Inquiry and Research Design: Choosing Among Five Approaches*. 2nd ed. Los Angeles: SAGE, 2007.

Creswell, John W, and J. David Creswell. *Research Design: Qualitative, Quantitative, and Mixed Methods Approaches*. Thousand Oaks, CA: SAGE, 2018. Kindle.

Creswell, John W., and Cheryl N. Poth. *Qualitative Inquiry and Research Design: Choosing Among Five Approaches*. Los Angeles: SAGE, 2018. Epub.

Crouch, Andy. *Culture Making: Recovering Our Creative Calling*. Downers Grove, IL: InterVarsity, 2008.

———. *The Tech-Wise Family: Everyday Steps for Putting Technology in Its Proper Place*. Grand Rapids: Baker, 2017. Epub.

Dasgupta, Partha. "Trust as a Commodity." In *Trust: Making and Breaking Cooperative Relations*, edited by Diego Gambetta, 49–72. New York: Basil Blackwell, 1998.

Delgado-Ballester, Elena, et al. "Development and Validation of a Brand Trust Scale." *International Journal of Market Research* 45 (2003) 35–53. https://doi.org/10.1177/147078530304500103.

Delio, Ilia. "Religion and Posthuman Life: Teilhard's Noosphere." In *Techno-Sapiens in a Networked Era: Becoming Digital Neighbors*, edited by Ryan K. Bolger and Kutter Callaway, 15–36. Eugene, OR: Cascade, 2020.

Dirks, Kurt D. "Three Fundamental Questions Regarding Trust in Leaders." In *Handbook of Trust Research*, edited by Reinhard Bachmann and Akbar Zaheer, 15–28. Cheltenham, UK: Elgar, 2008.

Doney, Patricia M., and Joseph P. Cannon. "An Examination of the Nature of Trust in Buyer-Seller Relationships." *Journal of Marketing* 61 (1997) 35–51. https://doi.org/10.1177/002224299706100203.

Doss, Gorden R. *Introduction to Adventist Mission*. Berrien Springs, MI: Seventh-day Adventist Theological Seminary, Andrews University, 2018. Kindle.

Dyer, John. *From the Garden to the City: The Redeeming and Corrupting Power of Technology*. Grand Rapids: Kregel, 2011. Scribd.

Ellison, Nicole B., et al. "The Benefits of Facebook 'Friends': Social Capital and College Students' Use of Online Social Network Sites." *Journal of Computer-Mediated Communication* 12 (2007) 1143–68. https://doi.org/10.1111/j.1083-6101.2007.00367.x.

Elliston, Edgar J. *Introduction to Missiological Research*. Pasadena: William Carey Library, 2011. Kindle.

Erikson, Erik H. *Childhood and Society*. New York: Norton, 1993.

Farmer, Thomas W., et al. "Social Dynamics Management: What Is It and Why Is It Important for Intervention?" *Journal of Emotional and Behavioral Disorders* 26 (2018) 3–10. https://doi.org/10.1177/1063426617752139.

Flick, Uwe. *Designing Qualitative Research*. Los Angeles: SAGE, 2014. Kindle.

———. *Managing Quality in Qualitative Research*. Qualitative Research Kit. Thousand Oaks, CA: SAGE, 2008.

Floridi, Luciano. *The Fourth Revolution: How the Infosphere Is Reshaping Human Reality*. Oxford: Oxford University Press, 2014.

Bibliography

Fowler, Floyd J. *Survey Research Methods*. 5th ed. Thousand Oaks, CA: SAGE, 2013.
Friesen, Dwight J. *Thy Kingdom Connected: What the Church Can Learn from Facebook, the Internet, and Other Networks*. Grand Rapids: Baker, 2009. Kindle.
Gambetta, Diego, ed. *Trust: Making and Breaking Cooperative Relations*. New York: Basil Blackwell, 1998.
Gertel, Jörg. "Uncertainty." In *Coping with Uncertainty: Youth in the Middle East and North Africa*, edited by Jörg Gertel and Ralf Hexel, loc. 591–1217. London: Saqi, 2018. Kindle.
———. "Youth in the MENA Region, 2016–17." In *Coping with Uncertainty: Youth in the Middle East and North Africa*, edited by Jörg Gertel and Ralf Hexel, loc. 144–579. London: Saqi, 2018. Kindle.
Gertel, Jörg, and Ralf Hexel, eds. *Coping with Uncertainty: Youth in the Middle East and North Africa*. London: Saqi, 2018. Kindle.
Gertel, Jörg, and David Kreuer. "Values." In *Coping with Uncertainty: Youth in the Middle East and North Africa*, edited by Jörg Gertel and Ralf Hexel, loc. 1236–1631. London: Saqi, 2018. Kindle.
Ghanem, Hafez. *The Arab Spring Five Years Later: Toward Great Inclusiveness*. Washington, DC: Brookings Institution, 2016. Kindle.
Gibbs, Graham R. *Analyzing Qualitative Data*. Los Angeles: SAGE, 2012. Kindle.
Glesne, Corrine. *Becoming Qualitative Researchers: An Introduction*. Boston: Allyn and Bacon, 2006.
Goriunova, Olga, and Chiara Bernardi. "Social Network Sites (SNSs)." In *The Johns Hopkins Guide to Digital Media*, edited by Marie-Laure Ryan et al., 456–62. Baltimore: Johns Hopkins University Press, 2014.
Gorrell, Angela Williams. *Always On: Practicing Faith in a New Media Landscape*. Theology for the Life of the World. Grand Rapids: Baker Academic, 2019.
Harlow, Summer. "It Was a 'Facebook Revolution': Exploring the Meme-Like Spread of Narratives During the Egyptian Protests." *Revista de Comunicación* 12 (2013) 59–82.
Hiebert, Paul G. *Transforming Worldviews: An Anthropological Understanding of How People Change*. Grand Rapids: Baker Academic, 2009. Kindle.
Howard, Philip N., and Muzammil M. Hussain. *Democracy's Fourth Wave? Digital Media and the Arab Spring*. New York: Oxford University Press, 2013. Kindle.
Husserl, Edmund. *The Essential Husserl: Basic Writings in Transcendental Phenomenology*. Edited by Donn Welton. Bloomington: Indiana University Press, 1999.
Ipsos. "MENA's Millennials Decoded." *Ipsos*, September 10, 2018. https://www.ipsos.com/en/menas-millennials-decoded.
Jick, Todd D. "Mixing Qualitative and Quantitative Methods: Triangulation in Action." *Administrative Science Quarterly* 24 (1979) 602–11.
Kim, Kirsteen. "Missiology Lectures 2019: Techno-Sapiens in a Networked Era." Presented at the Missiology Lectures 2019, Fuller Seminary, October 31, 2019. https://youtu.be/D3G9lbR2s14.
Kirk, Jerome, and Marc L. Miller. *Reliability and Validity in Qualitative Research*. Thousand Oaks, CA: SAGE, 1985. Kindle.
Kogut, Bruce Mitchel. *The Global Internet Economy*. Cambridge: MIT Press, 2003.
Kolb, Darl G., et al. "Connectivity and Leadership: The Influence of Online Activity on Closeness and Effectiveness." *Journal of Leadership and Organizational Studies* 15 (2009) 342–52. https://doi.org/10.1177/1548051809331503.

Bibliography

Komiak, Sherrie Y. X., and Izak Benbasat. "The Effects of Personalization and Familiarity on Trust and Adoption of Recommendation Agents." *MIS Quarterly* 30 (2006) 941–60. https://doi.org/10.2307/25148760.

Kraft, Charles H. *Communicating Jesus' Way*. Pasadena: Carey, 2013.

Kramer, Roderick M., and Tom R. Tyler. *Trust in Organizations: Frontiers of Theory and Research*. Thousand Oaks, CA: SAGE, 1999.

Kvale, Steinar. *Doing Interviews*. Los Angeles: SAGE, 2012. Kindle.

Laeequddin, Mohammed, et al. "Trust Building in Supply Chain Partners Relationship: An Integrated Conceptual Model." *Journal of Management Development* 31 (2012) 550–64. https://doi.org/10.1108/02621711211230858.

Lastrucci, C. L. *The Scientific Approach: Basic Principles of the Scientific Method*. Cambridge: Schenkman, 1967.

Leedy, Paul D., and Jeanne Ellis Ormrod. *Practical Research: Planning and Design, Global Edition*. Edinburgh: Pearson Education, 2015. Kindle.

Lewicki, Roy J., and Barbara Benedict Bunker. "Trust in Relationships: A Model of Development and Decline." In *Conflict, Cooperation, and Justice: Essays Inspired by the Work of Morton Deutsch*, edited by Barbara Benedict Bunker and Jeffrey Zachary Rubin, 133–74. San Francisco: Jossey-Bass, 1995.

Lindgren, Simon, et al. "Hybrid Media Culture." In *Hybrid Media Culture: Sensing Place in a World of Flows*, edited by Simon Lindgren, 1–15. New York: Routledge, 2013.

Ling, Richard Seyler, and Jonathan Donner. *Mobile Communication*. Cambridge: Polity, 2009.

Luhmann, Niklas. "Familiarity, Confidence, Trust: Problems and Alternatives." In *Trust: Making and Breaking Cooperative Relations*, edited by Diego Gambetta, 94–108. New York: Basil Blackwell, 1998.

Mahfouz, Asmaa. "Asmaa Mahfouz and the YouTube Video That Helped Spark the Egyptian Uprising." *Democracy Now!*, February 8, 2011. http://www.democracynow.org/2011/2/8/asmaa_mahfouz_the_youtube_video_that.

Manovich, Lev. *The Language of New Media*. Cambridge: MIT Press, 2001.

Mayer, Roger C., et al. "An Integrative Model of Organizational Trust." *Academy of Management Review* 20 (1995) 709–34. https://doi.org/10.5465/amr.1995.9508080335.

McKnight, D. Harrison, and Norman L. Chervany. "Reflections on an Initial Trust-Building Model." In *Handbook of Trust Research*, edited by Reinhard Bachmann and Akbar Zaheer, 29–51. Cheltenham, UK: Elgar, 2008.

Mehdizadeh, Soraya. "Self-Presentation 2.0: Narcissism and Self-Esteem on Facebook." *Cyberpsychology, Behavior, and Social Networking* 13 (2010) 357–64. https://doi.org/10.1089/cyber.2009.0257.

Meyerson, Debra E., et al. "Swift Trust and Temporary Groups." In *Trust in Organizations: Frontiers of Theory and Research*, edited by Roderick M. Kramer and Tom R. Tyler, 261–87. Thousand Oaks, CA: SAGE, 1996.

Michalos, Alex C. *How Good Policies and Business Ethics Enhance Good Quality of Life: The Selected Works of Alex C. Michalos*. Cham: Springer International, 2017. https://doi.org/10.1007/978-3-319-50724-8.

Milton-Edwards, Beverley. *Marginalized Youth: Toward an Inclusive Jordan*. Washington, DC: Brookings Institution, 2018. https://think-asia.org/handle/11540/8351.

Bibliography

Mishra, Aneil K. "Oganizational Responses to Crisis: Centrality of Trust." In *Trust in Organizations: Frontiers of Theory and Research*, edited by Roderick M. Kramer and Tom R. Tyler, 261–87. Thousand Oaks, CA: SAGE, 1996.

Morgan, David L. *Focus Groups as Qualitative Research*. Thousand Oaks, CA: SAGE, 1996. Kindle.

Moustakas, Clark. *Phenomenological Research Methods*. Thousand Oaks, CA: SAGE, 2010.

Moysidou, Krystallia, and J. Piet Hausberg. "In Crowdfunding We Trust: A Trust-Building Model in Lending Crowdfunding." *Journal of Small Business Management* 58 (2020) 511–43. https://doi.org/10.1080/00472778.2019.1661682.

Mumford, Lewis. *Technics and Civilization*. New York: Harcourt, Brace, and Company, 1934.

Myers, Bryant L. *Engaging Globalization: The Poor, Christian Mission, and Our Hyperconnected World*. Grand Rapids: Baker Academic, 2017. Kindle.

Ouaissa, Rachid. "Religion." In *Coping with Uncertainty: Youth in the Middle East and North Africa*, edited by Jörg Gertel and Ralf Hexel, loc. 1637–1952. London: Saqi, 2018. Kindle.

Paparoidamis, Nicholas G., et al. "The Role of Supplier Performance in Building Customer Trust and Loyalty: A Cross-Country Examination." *Industrial Marketing Management* 78 (2019) 183–97. https://doi.org/10.1016/j.indmarman.2017.02.005.

Punch, Keith. *Survey Research the Basics*. Thousand Oaks, CA: SAGE, 2003.

Putnam, Robert D. *Bowling Alone: The Collapse and Revival of American Community*. New York: Touchstone, 2001.

Rea, Louis M., and Richard Allen Parker. *Designing and Conducting Survey Research: A Comprehensive Guide*. San Francisco: Jossey-Bass, 2014.

Rheingold, Howard. *The Virtual Community: Homesteading on the Electronic Frontier*. Cambridge: MIT Press, 2000.

Rogers, Everett M. *Diffusion of Innovations*. New York: Free, 2003. Epub.

Rotter, Julian B. "A New Scale for the Measurement of Interpersonal Trust." *Journal of Personality* 35 (1967) 651–65. https://doi.org/10.1111/j.1467-6494.1967.tb01454.x.

Rousseau, Denise M., et al. "Not So Different After All: A Cross-Discipline View of Trust." *Academy of Management Review* 23 (1998) 393–404. https://doi.org/10.5465/amr.1998.926617.

Rubin, Herbert J., and Irene Rubin. *Qualitative Interviewing: The Art of Hearing Data*. Thousand Oaks, CA: SAGE, 2012.

Ruel, Erin, et al. *Practice of Survey Research: Theory and Applications*. Thousand Oaks, CA: SAGE, 2016. Epub.

Rushkoff, Douglas. *Program or Be Programmed: Ten Commands for a Digital Age*. New York: OR, 2010.

Ryan, Marie-Laure, et al., eds. *The Johns Hopkins Guide to Digital Media*. Baltimore: Johns Hopkins University Press, 2014.

Sathyanesan, Shyju. "Internet Evangelism: A Web Ministry to Reach Internationals at International Ministries, Springfield." DMin diss., Assemblies of God Theological Seminary, 2019.

Schein, Edgar H. *Organizational Culture and Leadership*. 5th ed. New York: Wiley, 2016.

Schultze, Quentin J. "Following Pilgrims into Cyberspace." In *Understanding Evangelical Media: The Changing Face of Christian Communication*, edited by Quentin J. Schultze and Robert Herbert Woods Jr. Downers Grove, IL: IVP Academic, 2009. Kindle.

Bibliography

Schultze, Quentin J., and Robert Herbert Woods Jr., eds. *Understanding Evangelical Media: The Changing Face of Christian Communication*. Downers Grove, IL: IVP Academic, 2009. Kindle.

Schwartz, Sarah E. O., et al. "Mentoring in the Digital Age: Social Media Use in Adult-Youth Relationships." *Children and Youth Services Review* 47 (2014) 205–13. https://doi.org/10.1016/j.childyouth.2014.09.004.

Schwarz, Christoph H. "Family and the Future." In *Coping with Uncertainty: Youth in the Middle East and North Africa*, edited by Jörg Gertel and Ralf Hexel, loc. 2272–565. London: Saqi Books, 2018. Kindle.

Shaw, R. Daniel. "Qualitative Social Science Methods in Research Design." In *Introduction to Missiological Research*. Pasadena, CA: William Carey, 2011. Kindle.

Søgaard, Viggo. *Research in Church and Mission*. Pasadena: Carey, 1996.

Turkle, Sherry. *Alone Together: Why We Expect More from Technology and Less from Each Other*. New York: Basic, 2011. Epub.

United Nations Development Programme. "Arab Human Development Report 2016: Youth and the Prospects for Human Development in Changing Reality." Executive Summary. Lebanon: United Nations Development Programme, Regional Bureau for Arab States, 2016. https://www.arabstates.undp.org/content/rbas/en/home/library/huma_development/arab-human-development-report-2016—youth-and-the-prospects-for-.html.

Valkenburg, Patti M., and Jochen Peter. "Social Consequences of the Internet for Adolescents: A Decade of Research." *Current Directions in Psychological Science* 18 (2009) 1–5. https://doi.org/10.1111/j.1467-8721.2009.01595.x.

Vannini, Phillip, et al. "Toward a Technography of Everyday Life: The Methodological Legacy of James W. Carey's Ecology of Technoculture as Communication." *Cultural Studies ↔ Critical Methodologies* 9 (2009) 462–76. https://doi.org/10.1177/1532708609332424.

Whitener, Ellen M., et al. "Managers as Initiators of Trust: An Exchange Relationship Framework for Understanding Managerial Trustworthy Behavior." *Academy of Management Review* 23 (1998) 513–30. https://doi.org/10.5465/amr.1998.926624.

www.ingramcontent.com/pod-product-compliance
Lightning Source LLC
Chambersburg PA
CBHW051737230426
43670CB00012B/2062